Eclectic Eco-Concerns

IN STEPHEN GILL'S POETRY

Eclectic Eco-Concerns

IN STEPHEN GILL'S POETRY

Eclectic Eco-Concerns

IN STEPHEN GILL'S POETRY

Nar Deo Sharma

AUTHORSPRESS

Worldwide Circulation through Authorspress Global Network
First Published in 2022
by
Authorspress
Q-2A Hauz Khas Enclave, New Delhi-110 016 (India)
Phone: (0) 9818049852
E-mail: authorspressgroup@gmail.com
Website: www.authorspressbooks.com

Eclectic Eco-Concerns in Stephen Gill's Poetry
ISBN 978-93-5529-165-3

Printed in India at Thomson Press (India) Limited

For my dearest grandson
Rudransh Sharma
who helped me multifariously

Contents

Preface

Nar Deo Sharma's *Eclectic Eco-Concerns in Stephen Gill's Poetry* is a highly original work that significantly contributes to the growing body of Stephen Gill scholarship, particularly in its ecocritical methodology, enhanced by his incorporation of literary stylistics. One of the most distinctive and powerful aspects of this book is its application of Stephen Gill's poetic concerns with terrorism – the "destruction caused by maniac messiahs" – to contemporary historical events, in particular the brutalities of ISIS and the Taliban, with repeated references to Black Tuesday, when 132 schoolchildren were butchered at the Army Public School in Pakistan. The reader is reminded how truly prescient Gill has been in his literary preoccupation with terrorism, growing out of his own traumatic experiences following the Partition of India.[1] This prescience carries with it a growing urgency when, in his introduction to Dr. Sharma's book, Gill observes that the "grains of humanism and humaneness" are wearing off in modern people.

What makes Stephen Gill's eco-concerns "eclectic"? One need only look at the divisions in the Table of Contents – referencing social, political, religious, nature, and human ecology – to appreciate Dr. Sharma's wide-ranging investigation of Gill's eco-concerns. We might want to pause, however, to consider what exactly makes Stephen Gill an ecopoet as opposed to, say, a nature poet.

John Shoptaw, in responding to the question posed in the title of his well-known essay "Why Ecopoetry?", states that the answer is two-fold: "an ecopoem needs to be environmental and it needs to be environmentalist." Shoptaw explains, "By environmental, I mean first

---

1 In his autobiographical account of the effects of the Partition, Gill has written, "It was a shock when I realised that the darkness I left benind had been chasing me continuously." The thought of cruelty of humans always remained in my mind like my own shadow. The more I thought of it, the more I became obsessed to write about it. (qtd. in *Discovering Stephen Gill*, p. x).

that an ecopoem needs to be about the non-human natural world – wholly or partly, in some way or other, but really and not just figuratively.... an ecopoem is a kind of nature poem. But an ecopoem needs more than the vocabulary of nature."

Shoptaw's explanation of his second criterion for an ecopoem is particularly relevant to Stephen Gill's eco-concerns. He writes,

> An ecopoem must be not only environmental but environmentalist. First, the environment of an ecopoem is, implicitly or explicitly, impacted by humans. As Ursula K. Heise puts it, ecopoetry is 'related to the broader genre of nature poetry but can be distinguished from it by the portrayal of nature as threatened by human activities.'

Shoptaw concludes,

> An ecopoem is environmentalist not only thematically, in that it represents environmental damage or risk, but rhetoricially: it is urgent, and it aims to unsettle.

This definition beautifully segues into Nar Deo Sharma's exploration of the poetics of Stephen Gill's "eclectic eco-concerns." By applying literary sylistics to Gill's poetry,[2] he demonstrates how Gill's imagery, figurative language, and poetic techiques, in particular alliteration, wed his form to his content, addressing not only the damage that humans are inflicting upon the earth through their cupidity and twisted ideologies, but also the urgency to do something about this. (In Stephen Gill's writing, from the beginning, this quest has been his expressed in his devotion to World Federalism and global peace.)

And Gill *aims* to unsettle. Concomitant with his belief in universal brotherhood and sisterhood and the solace of the natural world is his acute awareness of the depravity and cruelty of human beings, as in his representation of the fanaticism and irrationality of terrorists in Canto 27 of *The Flame*:

> Who can tell how they felt
> tormenting the bird of peace
> with the cigarette lighter of their lust
> or the butt of the rifle of their bigotry. (93)

Sharma has observed in his recent article "Ekphrastic Poetry on Terrorism" that the last two lines of this stanza "shine with the magic

---

2 M.H. Abrams notes that these sylistic features "may be phonological (patterns of speech sounds, meter, or rhyme), or syntactic (types of sentence structure), or lexical (abstract vs. concrete words, the relative frequency of nouns, verbs, adjectives) or rhetorical (the characteristics of figurative language, imagery, and so on)" (*A Glossary of Literary Terms*, pp. 305-6).

of neology. Multi-layered message is encapsulated in the innovative metaphoric phrase 'the cigarette lighter of their lust.'"

Here Gill's employment of figurative language and alliteration (a sound device that some critics view as a type of figurative language in its heightening of mood and enhancement of imagery) suggests why he instinctively turns to poetry to unsettle his readers: the stanza's vivid images of cruelty and barbarism are intensified through metaphor and alliteration, the tormented bird of peace in itself a figurative name for a dove.

Yet *The Flame* also comforts Gill's readers in later cantos that display a Schweitzerian reverence for life and passionate commitment to global peace, as in these lines from canto #60:

> Where the dove flies without fear
> and the lilies of justice
> blossom for all
> that domain of yours
> assures a comforting niche
> for the songs I write
> for you. (146)

Here the Bird of Peace reappears free of torment.

In his preface to *Songs Before Shrine*, Stephen Gill has observed,

> I believe that the language of poetry is more compact, energetic, of greater intensity and emotional depth than the language of prose is, and it has no room for cliches and unnecessary words. Poetry is a villa of glorious shapes where every brick that is chiselled in a unique way belongs to an exact spot. (vii)

In viewing Gill's eco-concerns through the lens of literary sylistics, Nar Deo Sharma has illuminated and painstakingly detailed the poetic strategies that Stephen Gill has enlisted in unsettling his readers through his vision of "disgusting social ecology, depraved political ecology, and nasty religious ecology," countering these with "decent nature ecology and virtuous human ecology." His sensitive and insightful reading of Gill's poetic texts is supported by a distinctive critical methodology that foregrounds Stephen Gill's highly original poetics while confirming his significant contribution to the genre of ecopoetry.

Dr. Daniel Bratton
Coordinator of Humanities, Culture and Language Studies
Renison University College, University of Waterloo, Canada

Ekphrastic Poetry on Terrorism

The salient attributes of *ekphrastic poetry* are manifest in Dr. Stephen Gill's poems published in his outstanding book – The Flame. In a nutshell, the term *ekphrastic originates from a Greek expression for description.* By means of an effusive use of details, writers in ancient Greece aspired to transform the visual into the verbal. For example, Book 18 of The Iliad (ca. 762 BC) includes lengthy detailed description of the shield that Achilles carried. Horace coined the formula: ut pictura poesis *(as is painting, so is poetry),* drawing aphorism attributed to Simonides of Ceos by Plutarch, who praised historians for their lively prose that made readers see actions described in words.

> In the Glossary of Poetic Terms (poetryfoundation.org), the word ekphrasis means: "Description" in Greek. An ekphrastic poem is a vivid description of a scene or, more commonly, a work of art. Through the imaginative act of narrating and reflecting on the "action" of a painting or sculpture, the poet may amplify and expand its meaning. A notable example is "Ode on a Grecian Urn", in which the poet John Keats speculates on the identity of the lovers who appear to dance and play music, simultaneously frozen in time in perpetual motion."

Timothy Green – Editor of famous American magazine: Rattle (rattle.com) administers a regular paid feature namely, *Ekphrastic Poetry Challenge.* He pores over the characteristics of ekphrastic poetry in this way: "*Hi Nar – As I use the word and it's come to be understood, ekphrasis is a written description/ response to a piece of art work. So reverse ekphrastic poetry would be reversing that, and have a painting or some other type of art created on a poem. We've done these with poems at our literary festival.*"

Unlike Homer, Horace, Plutarch and others, *Stephen Gill* dispenses with the objects of eye-feasting paintings, golden pot, sculpture or a piece of art work in his poems, but then *his ekphrastic poems showcase the heart-wringing specimens of human detritus – the leftovers of human dead bodies and their cut-limbs that testify to the maelstrom of massacre perpetrated by the inhuman terrorists electrified by the vicious vibes of Muslim fanaticism.*

Thematic crux of Gill's ekphrastic poems enlightens us that eclectic eco-concerns signify poet's vehement poetic protests against the inhuman atrocities committed by the fanatic terrorists that he has expressed in various CANTOS at great length in his outstanding epic – *The Flame (2008).*

The poet pours his anguished feelings about terrorists in these words: *"The maniac messiahs open Pandora's box with the fingers of science and technology, using the muscles of fanaticism to spread the dust of untold brutalities for the sake of their macabre pleasure. "Their path to that domain is paved with the bones of the children and painted with the blood of the innocents. The flowers that grow on both sides of that path are fed with the tears of the hopeless children and widows. "December 16, 2014 will be the unprecedented BLACK TUESDAY in the history of inhumanity as TALIBANI terrorists shot 132 school children in the Army School of Pakistan."*

In order to hone up the creativity of readers to appreciate individually the linguistic subtleties and emotive appeal vividly that beautify ekphrastic poems, I cite a few exemplary ekphrastic poems, namely *Cantos* culled from – The Flame that testify to the depraved facets of heinous crimes perpetrated by the terrorists on children and peace-loving people. *It is noteworthy that Gill adorns his poems with nonpareil arrays of astute poetic devices that glitter in amazing neological phrases, innovative metaphors, symbolic imagery and connotative nuances for the sake of intensifying the indelible relish of smarting sensibilities embedded in ekphrastic poems.* In the poem: Canto-27 (*The Flame, p.93)* irrational hatred of terrorists seething with fanaticism is questioned through the artistic beauty of neologism:

> Who can tell how they felt
> tormenting the bird of peace
> with the cigarette lighter of their lust
> or the butt of the rifle of their bigotry

In the last two sentences bearing the magic of neology, it is presupposed that terrorists not only raped innocent girls, burnt their thighs to quench the rage of their sadistic ugly mindset but pierced their thighs with the rifle butts of fanaticism.

In the catalogue poem: Canto-22 (The Flame, p.78), the poet has described vividly the massive killings by the fanatic terrorists:

> shocked volunteers/ witnessed a pyramid of ashes
> over the cradles/ a bone chilling calculation
> that demeaned the design in living.
> there was no wailing, no screaming
> over the earth shattering slaughter
> that pulverized the leaves/ of the young season
> through the openings of the burial cabin

time differently watches/ the ethical poverty of the zealots
who frenzied on the wildness of malice.

In the above catalogue poem, the poet has *vividly portrayed the ugly facets of disgusting human ecology.* The metaphoric phrase, *"a pyramid of ashes over the cradles"* implies the agonising nuance of massive carnage of innocent children. The glint of symbolic imagery in the metaphoric phrase *"pulverized leaves of the young season"* connotes widespread slaughter of the teenagers by the cruel terrorists.

Other catalogue poem: Canto-20 an extract from the book, *The Flame, p.72,* unravels the cumulative outrage of the ghoulish terrorists that peaks in the carnage of innocent children:

With jackhammers and chainsaws
they removed the obstacles
to dig out the nursery
buried under a pile of rubble.

In the above poem, the noun phrase, the nursery, symbolises innocent children killed by the malignant terrorists who were obsessed with fanaticism. *When the poet perceives the amoral mindset of terrorists, he finds them bad conductors of mercy and grossly insulated against affections. Little children for them are but the trivial objects of killing rather than love.*

On the whole, Dr. Stephen Gill is not confined only to composing ugly ekphrastic poems on the grisly crimes committed by inhuman terrorists, but he contemplates also the dawn of virtuous human ecology which is scented with compassion, true love, fraternity, peace and these humane ideals the poet ensures in these lines teeming with unflinching optimism of Canto-60 contained in *The Flame*, p.146:

Where creeds are not crushed
and human gods do not feed
the vultures of war
that island of yours
defends the dignity of freedoms
are distinctive and charming.

I hope dear readers, critics, poets and reviewers will tickle me with their joy after reading my critique on the novel genre of ekphrastic poetry.

Nar Deo Sharma

Works Cited

Abrams, M.H. *A Glossary of Literary Terms / Seventh Edition.* Heinle & Heinle, 1999.

Agarwal, Nilanshu Kumar, ed. D*iscovering Stephen Gill: A Collection of Papers and Articles.* Authorspress, 2008.

Gill, Stephen. *The Flame.* Vesta Publications Canada, 2008.

.... *Songs Before Shrine.* Authorspress, 2007.

Shoptaw, John. "Why Ecopoetry?" Why Ecopoetry? by John Shoptaw | Poetry Magazine (poetryfoundation.org).

Sharma, Nar Deo. "Stephen Gill's Ekphrastic Poetry on Terrorism."

Foreword

I met Dr. Nar Sharma about a decade ago when I visited Rajasthan as one of the PhD examiners of his thesis.

In those days there was no provision for plagiarism check and I had to go through the thesis very carefully to point out repetition etc. Stephen Gill, on whom the thesis was written, happened to be my close friend and I too have edited a full length book on him. *Dr Nar Sharma had exhaustively and deeply read Gill's poems and pointed out even those aspects of his poetry which were not known to me.* When I was to return from that memorable journey, Dr Sharma presented me his collections of poems. Since then he has richly contributed to the world of poetry. I read the collections that he had gifted me and waited for more which I got, I think, a couple of years back.

I too, at times, attempt at creative writing but my favourite area is fiction and do not read contemporary poets, until it is absolutely necessary.

Dr Sharma's case was different as he developed very close academic relations with me as the time passed. Unlike many modern Indian poets writing in English, Sharm's poetry is deeply rooted in soil and comes straight from the deepest corners of his heart hence it directly descends in the heart of readers. His pen dances to his heart's tune in such a manner that the reader can easily connect himself with the emotional roller coaster of his poesy. He is the clearest and most impressive Voice of Rajasthan whose poetry one can listen to the enchanting melody and rhythm of Rajasthani folk life.

It is noteworthy that Dr Sharma has pioneered an unprecedented scholarly research work titled above on Dr Gill's nonpareil, contemporary ekphrastic poetry on terrorism that dwarfs the impact as well as the utility of traditional ekphrastic poetry based on the vivid description of the work of art.

Professor I.D. Tiwari
Former Head, Dept of English
Central University Guru Ghasidas, Bilaspur CG, Registrar
IK SV Khairagarh

Introduction by Stephen Gill

Dr. Nar Deo Sharma's doctoral dissertation has clarity of vision, logical development, acceptable language and his findings are noteworthy. He has taken time and efforts to dive deeply into the sea of data analysis and stylistic devices. I find these chapters and extensive bibliography certainly impressive. He states the purpose of his dissertation clearly.

I knew Nar Deo Sharma even before he was registered for his doctoral dissertation, titled *Eclectic Eco Concerns in Stephen Gill's Poetry*. His name came to my attention once in a while. I wrote a review of the collection of his poems *Melody of Wounds*. This collection, free from cliché, has fresh imagery. I would like to add that his doctoral dissertation is written almost in the same spirit.

In his research work Nar Deo Sharma focusses on eco concerns in Stephen Gill's poetry, particularly on perverse human ecology. He clarifies his stand in the first chapter of his research work:

> Eclectic eco-concerns of the poet are relevant to the perverse human ecology which is accountable for multifold ecocide. The perverse human ecology is entrenched in amoral mindset and immoral deeds of people. The poet has unfolded that the perverse human ecology is an amalgam of disgusting social ecology, depraved political ecology and nasty religious ecology of the terrorists that has been outraging the natural ecology. Stephen Gill is a diasporic, Canadian poet, and the study of his ecocentric poetry is relevant to the genre of eco-criticism.

The researcher's main reason for selecting certain collections and certain poems from these collections is obvious from the lines quoted below. About these Stephen Gill's certain poems Dr. Sharma in one of his articles states:

> ...significant poems from different poetry books have been gleaned for study that have bearing on poet's eclectic eco-concerns. Peace, fraternity, moral values in every walk of life, propagation of the religion of love and protection of nature ecology are the key image-motifs prevailing in the poems. It is noteworthy that images stripped of motifs seem to be merely word pictures that do not wake emotions. Image clusters demonstrate the

abundance of various emotions, such as, love, hate, anger, jealousy, hope and others. Various image clusters coalesce to render manifold connotations of vivid feelings ingrained in poems.

He points out that eclectic eco-concerns testify to diverse crimes perpetrated by terrorists that encompass facets of perverse human ecology, including social, political and religious. He also points out that the grains of humanism are shrinking day by day. He argues that canto 20 from *The Flame* is filled with the cumulative outrage of terrorists that culminates in the carnage of children:

With jackhammers and chainsaws
they removed obstacles
to dig out the nursery
buried under a pile of rubble.
No little hands reached them.
Only tiny voices
and faint sobs they heard.
They saw babies
shrouded in blood
and…

This canto 20 displays picturesque facets of depraved political ecology. Here nursery symbolises innocent children killed by the inhuman elements who were obsessed with their depraved political ecology.

Another canto worth mentioning here is number 27, also from *The Flame*. Dr. Sharma finds multifold facets of religious ecology in this canto:

Who can tell if the night before/ they tied and untied the knots of reason before plunging the bayonets/ into the raw flesh to appease Beelzebub with their offerings at the altar/ of their seething cauldron of wrath who can tell how/ they felt when they concealed the carcass of their rusted notions/ under the rock of the blinding luster of the gold of their creed.

The significant lines: "*who can tell…..the gold of their creed*" reveals the truth that very poor, illiterate and unemployed young persons are often allured by the agents of Beelzebub. There is a nuanced foregrounding in the metaphoric phrase "*the carcass of rusted notions*" in that the young agents of terrorism carry away their dead soul on the hearse of fanaticism. Obviously terrorism is the destructive creed propagated by the followers of Beelzebub, founded on the path of allurement, coercion, hatred, massacre and antagonism to other religions.

Number 30 is another canto that attracts the researcher. Addressed to mothers, this canto displays the gruesome facets of perverse human ecology:

> Mothers do not weep
> .....
> Shed your tears with cries/ from the skies of your fond memories
> to awake their conscience/ slumbering in the shambles of brutality.
> Offer your hymns to a new birth.

The canto is about the ineffable agonies of mothers. It refers to their cries and the conscience of terrorists who derive immense pleasures in the merciless killings of children. The innovative metaphoric phrase "*conscience slumbering in the shambles of brutality*" implies that brutality is ingrained in the mindset of the terrorists, and it shambles in their conscience.

The violent facet of disgusting social ecology is portrayed in the imagery in Canto 43:

> I see a deer chased/ by a tiger who is fed
> on the flaunting fruits of terror/ in the bushes of
> unparalleled ignorance/ where he cannot hear
> the birds of freedom

The researcher says that the lines above are enriched with the animal imagery to unfold the shameful birth of terrorism. Beautiful symbolic referents are employed to demonstrate the malignant inhuman ecology of the terrorists. Deer signifies an innocent, timid and moneyless youth, while tiger typifies a barbaric leader of the assassins of humanity. The alliterative phrase *flaunting fruits* connotes tempting prospects leading to terrorism. In the prepositional phrase: *in the bushes of ignorance* modified by an adjective phrase: *unparalleled ignorance,* specify the semantic rule of violation of selection restrictions in detail is violated which is analysed here. In addition, the phrase – *the bushes of ignorance* signifies the illiteracy of the youths who are tempted and coerced to indulge in murderous activities of the terrorists resulting in gross ecocide.

I would like to quote Professor RC Shukla's opinion on *The Flame* that the researcher has selected for his study. In addition to research papers by university professors, a book was edited by an established literary critic Professor Dr. Sudhir K. Arora, titled *The Flame Unmasked* that was released in 2010 by Prakash Book Depot, a prominent publisher of India. *The Flame, m*odern epic, is about the destruction caused by maniac messiahs. I have used the word maniac messiahs for religious terrorists. R.C. Shukla is a respectable poet, literary critic and a professor who has taught English Literature for years and supervised doctoral candidates. He states in "The Speculative Solemnity in Stephen Gill's *The Flame*", published in *The Flame Unmasked:*

> Extremely rich in symbolism and the use of imagery, Gill's poem is an evidence of his astonishing merits as a poet. The use of new adjectives and nouns from the beginning to the end is sure to establish Stephen Gill as a poet par excellence. It is certain that no poet of England wrote poetry with such a rich stock of imagery except John Milton in his Paradise Lost and Samson Agnostes. Even the exceedingly romantic poet Shelley who wrote Prometheus Unbound has in this particular sense, been defeated by this great Canadian poet. (p.9).

Several research papers on *The Flame* have been published in university journals and literary studies. Nar Deo Sharma in his dissertation says about *The Flame:*

> In order to reduce the redundancy of appraisal, I cite a few exemplary ekphrastic poems, namely Cantos culled from – The Flame that testify to the depraved facets of heinous crimes perpetrated by the terrorists on children and peace-loving people. It is noteworthy that Gill adorns his poems with nonpareil array of astute poetic devices that glitter in amazing neological phrases, innovative metaphors, symbolic imagery and connotative nuances for the sake of enhancing the relish of sensibilities embedded in ekphrastic poems.

I feel writing at least one short paragraph for every other book that Dr. Nar Deo Sharma has selected for his dissertation. I am afraid my introduction would become long, and unnecessary. Therefore I will write a paragraph only on *The Dove of Peace*. This collection was released first by M.A.F. Press from New York in 1989. Its introduction was written by John B. Lee, a multiple award-wining poet, Poet Laureate of Brantford, Ontario, and prominent poet of Canada. Below are a few lines from his introduction:

> Stephen Gill is a compassionate and intelligent writer and both of these strengths are reflected in The Dove of Peace. These poems express a longing for a time when all men will strive for a better world, but they are not unworldly poems. They recognise and name the presence of evil, though they dream of love. They strike a balance between knowledge of this world and the aspiration for a better one without becoming either cynical in the face of one reality, or naïve in their desire for an unachieved ideal….

I would like to add with pleasure that *The Dove of Peace* is an award-winning collection. This collection was recognised by Poetry in the Arts, Inc. on October 5, 1991 at "the Ninth Season of Poetry in the Arts, Incorporated, which is a non-profit forum for the presentation of international, national and local poets." Its founding directors General Edmunt C. Lynch, and Peggy Zuleika Lynch say in the certificate:

> Your publications, such as *The Dove of Peace*, provides leadership for world harmony through love. Your sensitivity to men's desire for a peaceful plant is a recurring theme in your poetry. Man's humanity to man advances imperceptibly. But the voices such as yours through the centuries plead for brotherhood. Often poetic appeal does cause man to pause even at times to stop to hear and try to effect peace. Your consistent appeal is therefore recognised with this award.

Coming back to ecology, the base of Dr. Sharma's dissertation, I am happy to note that the author has successfully completed the journey of the purpose of his research. I would like to quote a few lines from his last chapter, titled Conclusion:

> The poet makes sincere efforts through his strong poetic protests to revive virtuous human ecology to prevent multilayered ecocide. It is noteworthy that the existence of all living beings depends upon the safety, nourishment and preservation of Nature ecology in addition to enlightening the flame of peace, everlasting love and fraternity.

Before summarising my introduction I would like to look around to know what other literary critics have to say on the same subject. The critic that comes to my mind is Professor Dr. T. Ravichandran and his research paper "Green Dove: Ecoconcerns in Stephen Gill's *Shrine*", published in 2008 in Professor Dr. Nilanshu K. Agarwal's book *Discovering Stephen Gill*. Referring to Stephen Gill's collection *Shrine*, Professor T. Ravichandran on page 28-29 attests:

> Shrine is subtitled as Poems of Social Concerns; however, the whole collection can be viewed as "Poems of Ecological Concerns". At the outset, the author recalls in his preface where he shudders to remember the partition riots that he witnesses literally from close quarters. The human violence caused in mutual ill-will between the Hindus and the Muslims is also perceived as an act against nature. Or rather, it is nature that forebodes such violent happenings. Gill conjectures: every times there was a stir caused by the wind, a car on the street, the bark of a dog, or the mew of a cat, we froze inside our house. Later he observes that the city, New Delhi, smell rotten with the stench of the dead bodies…

Professor Dr. T. Ravichandran, author of the above lines, is of the opinion that most poems and the whole trauma of Stephen Gill during the partition of Panjab in 1947 is in ecological metaphors as if he was describing them as plants and other objects of nature. This is in line with what Nar Deo Sharma is doing in his particular way in his doctoral dissertation.

Nar Deo Sharma beautifully expresses foregrounding in his research paper "Significance of Foregrounding in Stephen Gill's Poetry" that appeared in Professor Dr. Shaleen Kumar Singh's book *Essays on the Poetry of Stephen Gill.* This book was released in 2010 by Adhyayan Publishers in New Delhi. Using the technique of foregrounding, Dr. Sharma says:

> Stephen Gill is a renowned, qualitative poet and his English poems stand out from that of other modern poets on account of foregrounding of intense sensibilities, precision of expression, creative imagination, symbolic use of language and liltingly vivid imagery. I have attempted to make an essay of various linguistic deviations that have enhanced the quality of poems compiled in his two poetry books: Songs Before Shrine (2007) and The Flame (2008).

I feel my introduction will remain incomplete without discussing a serious feature of *The Flame* because it is also the serious choice of the researcher. I have said in the first paragraph of my introduction that my understanding of the researcher was based on a couple of his articles I read here and there. A large part of this understanding was due to his skills in foregrounding. I thought that the dissertation was also about foregrounding. I do not read doctoral dissertations on Stephen Gill unless there is a special reason. This is not applicable to essays and research papers on Stephen Gill. Not only do I read and analyse articles and papers but also I keep copies in my file and often quote lines from them wherever there is their need. When Dr. Nar Deo Sharma, the researcher, informed me that his dissertation was accepted by a prominent publisher and he wanted me to write its introduction, I became more serious. I asked the researcher to send me a copy of his dissertation. Its reading opened a new vista for me.

I cannot express everything about this vista because of the nature of my introduction.

I am pleased to add that the researcher has made a judicious choice of the collections before *The Flame*. I bracket all those collections as my early work. These poems are short and the serious part that imagery, symbols and other poetic devices play in my later poetry starts with *The Flame*. This spectacular shift in my poetry is due to an epiphany I had during my literary tour to Texas and my discussion with a book publisher about Rabindranath Tagore, a Nobel Laureate. Actually my life is driven by epiphanies. For my literary voyage I do not have a guru or guide. I am not talking here about my subject. It has always been peace and related areas because of my early days in New Delhi. I am talking about my diction or style. The subject remained the same but its presentation differed. Symbols, metaphors and other poetic devices began to play an unusual part in my poetry from *The Flame*. The poems I wrote after *the Flame* include *Amputee*, *The Singer of Life* and now my Sufi sonnets – all longer poems.

This is the time to summarise with a few words the difficulties a successful doctoral candidate may face to have his or her dissertation published. Some universities put restrictions on their successful scholars to get their research works into the hands of book publishers. I do not support this practice because dissertations are the outcome of years of hard work under the supervision of experts. The work of these years of hard work should be made available widely to help junior scholars in many ways. Publication opens opportunities for the author of his or her work. Success of the book does not depend only on its academic quality. Publishers are in a highly competitive business. They look also for potential commercial value of the book. It is important that the book should have a larger appeal in some form. I congratulate Dr. Nar Deo Sharma for writing his successful doctoral dissertation and for finding a prominent book publisher to release it in book form for the benefit of researchers and general readers. I am sure they will benefit from the research of Dr. Nar Deo Sharma and his dedication to creative and critical literature.

Abstract

"Eclectic Eco-concerns" of the poet are relevant to the perverse human ecology which is accountable for multifold ecocide. The perverse human ecology is entrenched in amoral mindset and immoral deeds of people. *The poet has unfolded that the perverse human ecology is an amalgam of disgusting social ecology, depraved political ecology and nasty religious ecology of the fanatic terrorists that outrage decent nature ecology.* 21st century has to combat the crisis of ecocide due to vile ways of perverse human ecology. Stephen Gill is a renowned diasporic Canadian poet, and the study of his ecocentric poetry is connected with the genre of eco-criticism. The standpoints of the noted eco-critic Joseph W. Meeker (1997) are noteworthy in that: "Human beings are the earth's only literary creatures…If the creation of literature is an important characteristic of the human species, it should be examined carefully and honestly to discover its influence upon human behaviour and the natural environment to determine what role, if any, it plays in the welfare and survival of mankind."

1. Research objectives are intended to ascertain and analyse the causes of people's amoral mindset that propel them to spoil nature ecology. The thesis consists of descriptive research design, purposive judgment samplings, the technique and tools of stylistics for the interpretations of various connotations and emotive nuances foregrounded in the symbolic tropes of eco-centric poems. Unbelievable massacre of innocent children by the fanatic terrorists are explored by the poet in his epic: The Flame. *Overtaken by the extreme frenzy of Islamic fanaticism, the inhuman terrorists did out-Herod their vicious human ecology by shooting 132 innocent school children in the Army Public School in Pakistan on the Black Tuesday of 16 December 2014.* The poet concludes his poetic vision with an optimism for the dawn of a religion and a flame for true humanism and humaneness in the minds of vile people in fine tune with the Peace Nobel Laureate H.H. the Dalai Lama's preaching: "The purpose of our life needs to be positive. We weren't born

with the purpose of causing trouble, harms to others. For our life to be of value, I think we must develop basic human qualities…warmth, kindness, compassion. Then our life becomes meaningful, more peaceful…happier."

CHAPTER 1

Introduction

Eclectic eco-concerns of the poet are relevant to the perverse human ecology which is accountable for multifold ecocide. The perverse human ecology is entrenched in amoral mindset and immoral deeds of people. The poet has unfolded *that the perverse human ecology is an amalgam of disgusting social ecology, depraved political ecology and nasty religious ecology of the terrorists that has been outraging the natural ecology.* Stephen Gill is a diasporic, Canadian poet, and the study of his ecocentric poetry is relevant to the genre of *eco-criticism.*

M.H. Abrams (2008: p71) clarifies that "Eco-criticism (or by an alternate name, environmental criticism) designates the critical writings which explore the relation between literature and the biological and physical environment, conducted with an acute awareness of the devastation being wrought on that environment by human activities." 21st century is facing very acute problems of multifold damage of Nature ecology caused by mischievous human ecology.

Noted ecocritic Meeker (1974:p3-4) maintains that "Human beings are the earth's only literary creatures…If creation of literature is an important characteristic of the species, it should be examined carefully and honestly to discover its influence upon human behaviour and the natural environment…"

It is emphasized here that the fulfillment of nasty motives of malignant human ecology causes ecological hazards, such as, tropical warmth, acidifying of oceans, various severe cyclones, deforestation and murderous atrocities of the fanatic terrorists in particular. A good deal of ecological standpoints of noted ecocritics have been drawn from the The Ecocriticism Reader about which Abrams (2008:76) states: *"The anthology, The Ecocriticism Reader: Landmarks in Literary Ecology, ed. Cheryll Glotfelty and Harold Fromm (1996), did much, by its introduction and selections, to give definition and impetus to the ecocritical movement."* Ecology, as a branch of biology, deals with the reciprocal relationships between living organisms and their environment. Environment is an aggregate whole of all biotic (living) and abiotic (inorganic materials, water, soil etc.).

In the Fontana Dictionary of Modern Thought (1988:253), Kenneth Mellanby states that an ecosystem is "the system formed by the interaction of all living organisms, plants, animals, bacteria etc., with the physical and chemical factors of their environment." It is the malignant human ecology that is accountable for the disgusting violence, molestation, multi-layered corruption and extreme damage to the life-nurturing nature ecology. In Bullock's "Fontana Dictionary" (1988:33), Peter Hagget writes that the distinctive feature of human ecology is accordingly the attempt "to link the structure and organisation of a human community to interactions with its lacalised environment." It is apparent that to satisfy their nasty mercenary motives, the human tampering with the basic structure of nature and its natural courses has endangered biodiversity.

There is shocking degradation of the vital traits of humanism and humaneness among people these days that differentiate human beings from the wild animals.

Eisenberg in his book *Ecology of Eden* (1988:404) has rightly stated: "*The broad tendency of human meddling over the last ten thousand years has been to cut off flow within bioregions. Whatever we may be thinking, this is how we act: we flow globally and choke locally. Both ways, we reduce biodiversity.*"

Nasty human ecology which plays dominant role in the matter of massive ecocide is rooted in "*anthropocentrism*". M.H. Abrams(2008:72) explains the term in these words: "It is claimed that the reigning religions and philosophies of Western civilisation are deeply anthropocentric; that is, they are oriented to the interests of human beings, who are viewed as opposed to and superior to nature, and free to exploit natural resources and animal species for their own purpose."

On the contrary, Indian philosophy mainly based on the Vedas emphasises the worship of nature elements: water, planets, trees etc. Indian women have been the precursors of *eco-feminism* in that they worship Nature's elements, such as, peepal, banyan trees etc.

Works Cited

Abrams, M. H. (2008). *A Glossary of Literary Terms.8th ed.* New Delhi: Wadsworth Cengage Learning. pages:71, 72.

Bullock, A.O. Stallybrass and S. Trombley, eds. 1988. *The Fantana Dictionary of Modern Thought. 2nd ed.* London: Fontana.

Eisenberg, E. (1988*). Ecology of Eden.* New York: Alfred A. Knopf.

Glotfelty, C and Harold Fromm (eds.), *The Ecocriticism Reader: Landmarks in Literary Ecology.* (1996).Athens and London: University of Georgia Press.

Hagget, Peter. "Human Ecology," in Bullock et al (eds.). *The Fontana Dictionary of Modern Thought. 2nd ed.* London: Fontana. page 33.

Meeker, J. (1997). *The Comedy of Survival: Literary Ecology and the Play Ethic., 3rd edition.* Tuscan: University of Arizona Press. pages 3-4.

Mellanby, Kenneth. "Ecosystem," in Bullock et al (eds). *The Fontana Dictionary of Modern Thought.* 2nd ed. London: Fontana.

Rueckert, W. (1996). *Literature and Ecology: An Experiment in Ecocriticism,* in Glotfelty and Harold Fromm (eds.), *The Ecocriticism Reader: Landmarks in Literary Ecology.* Athens and London: University of Georgia Press. page 107.

CHAPTER 2

Objectives

The significant objectives defined as under are intended:

1. *to explore* different symbolic implications foregrounded in the poems that signify the destructive characteristics of perverse or malignant human ecology accountable for ecocide;
2. *to ascertain* the causes of amoral mindset of people that propels them to indulge in disgusting immoral deeds that spoil the purity of nature ecology;
3. *to explain* the various connotations and emotive nuances embedded in the symbolic language of eco-concerning poems;
4. *to analyze* the connection between figurative use of language and innovative standpoints that showcase the repulsive dynamics of immoral human ecology resulting in multilevel ecocide;
5. *to enlighten* people to enhance the life sustaining vitality of Nature ecology by means of refining upon the evil deeds.

Research Methodology

Methodology is a rational system of methods for the interpretation and evaluation of literary texts. According to Borev (1985:312), *'Method, i.e., the type of interpretational and evaluative operations and devices, ensures penetration into the object of investigation in order to reveal its anatomical structure, dissect the artistic text into elements and study each of them."*

In order to correspond with the thesis, *the methodology of stylistics* is employed to write up this literary research thesis. Stylistics is an element of linguistics, and linguistics is the systematic study of language. Stylistics plays very significant role in the interpretation of symbolic style in poetry. Turner (1977:07) in his book *Stylistics* differentiates the scope between linguistics and stylistics in these words: *'Linguistics is the science of describing language and showing how it*

and the description of its purpose and effect." All the stylistic features mentioned in Chapter 2 have been dealt in the different chapters of this book in order to interpret the symbolic messages and strong poetic protests against multilayered ecocide and erratic killings by the terrorists.

Works Cited

Borev, Yuri. (1985). *Aesthetics.* Moscow: Progress Publishers. page312.

Turner, G.W. (1977). *Stylistics.* Harmondsworth: Penguin Books. page 7.

Verdonk, Peter. (2014). *Stylistics.* Oxford: OUP. page 04.

CHAPTER 3

Stylistic Analysis

It is the distinctive style by which a poet stands out from others. Style is an aggregate of the distinctive linguistic choices systematised effectively in poetry. According to Noam Chomsky (1965:192) style is: *"style as choice* (choice of systematisation of select linguistic elements) *and style as deviation or unusual collocation."* Elaborating the features of style, Gleason (1965:428) writes: *"Style is the structuring of choices (choices of types of sentences, clauses, phrases, words, morphemes, tunes, images and graphological markers) made within the framework of a language and of literary forms."* Gill has coined innovative metaphors and symbolic imagery that, in the words of Leech et al (1990:16) *"involve both extra freedom (including freedom to depart from the rules of grammar), and extra discipline (the discipline which comes with the superimposition of special structure on language)."*

Here the departure from the rules of grammar refers to syntactic deviation, and the superimposition of structure on language pertains to semantic deviation or unusual collocation.

Stylistic analysis involves description, explication and evaluation of literary style. By means of stylistic analysis, the importance of linguistic deviations, foregrounding and violation of semantic rules of selection restrictions get justified as to how those devices contribute to symbolic use of language and add to the novelty of expression in poetry.

Stylistic Devices

An understanding of certain syntactic and semantic devices and their definitions enlighten the readers to interpret the implicit meanings and nuances embedded in poems. The poet shows predilection for picturesque imagery and symbolic expressions.

A symbol is defined in the Princeton Encyclopedia of Poetry and Poetics (1986) in these words: "*A literary symbol unites an image (the analogy) and an idea or conception (the subject) which that image suggests or evokes*". The significance of a symbol is emphasised in the Encyclopedia in these words: "*An idea which would be difficult, flat, lengthy or unmoving when expressed prosaically and big itself, may be made intelligible, vivid, economical and emotionally effective by use of symbols.*" The poet has made an effective use of metonymy in his poetry. Mostly, the critics skip metonymic phrases or words from factual interpretation, while implicit meanings are treasured in them.

Imagery is most important in creative and innovative poetry inasmuch as it renders great delight to our sense organs. Abrams (2008:129) elaborates upon the texture and impact of imagery in these words:

> "Imagery (that is, images taken collectively) is used to signify all the objects and quality of sense perception referred to in a poem or other work of literature, whether by literal description, by *allusion,* or in the *vehicles* (the secondary references) of its similes and metaphors…"

Abrams clarifies the scope of imagery in these words: "*Also, imagery in this usage includes not only visual sense qualities, but also qualities that are auditory, tactile (touch), thermal (heat and cold), olfactory (smell), gustatory (taste), and kinesthetic (sensations of movement).*" Modern critics stress that imagery is an essential component in poetry to enhance emotive effect, connotative meaning and innovative texture of the poetry.

Foregrounding is an exquisite and startling fusion of abstract and concrete thoughts that grips not only the attention of the readers but propels them to read the foregrounded lexical elements again and again. Verdonk (2014:118) defines foregrounding as *"The bringing of particular textual features into prominence, e.g. distinct patterns or parallelism, repetitions, and deviations from general linguistic rules or from the style."* The familiar matter is defamiliarised and common expression sounds remarkable in foregrounding. A remarkable linguistic artistry of the poet shines in the multilevel foregrounding in his poems.

Noted linguist Leech (1987:57) holds that "*deviations from linguistic or other social norms have been given the special name of foregrounding.*"

Linguistic deviation may be defined as the abnormal combinations of linguistic elements in violation of the conventions of language. Linguistic deviations are the phenomena of poetic devices. Gill's aim of introducing linguistic deviations in his poems is to foreground his unique experience which cannot be described in ordinary language effectively.

According to Chomsky (1965:153), the degrees of deviations are: "*a violation of lexical category (lexical deviation), conflict with a strict subcategorisation feature (grammatical deviation), and a conflict with a selectional feature (semantic deviation).*"

The characteristic features of linguistic deviations or multilevel foregrounding and their effectiveness are examined further in relevant chapters in context of poems. It is discerned that the poems composed by Stephen Gill exhibit his keen predilection for *neology* connected with lexical deviations that attract the violation of the semantic rules of selection restrictions.

The detailed interpretation and relevant explanations regarding *Neology* and innovative figurative use of language are discussed in next chapters. In so many poems, the poet has rendered music in his poetry by means of *assonance and alliteration.*

Works cited

Abrams, M.H. (2008) 8th ed. *A Glossary of Literary Terms.* New Delhi: Wadsworth Cengage Learning. page: 129.

Chomsky, Noam. (1965). *Aspects of the Theory of Syntax.* Cambridge, Mass: MIT Press. pages: 153, 192.

Gleason, H.A. (1965). *Linguistics and English Grammar.* New York: Holt, Rinehart & Wilson. page: 428.

Leech, Geoffrey N. (1987) 12th imp. *A Linguistic Guide to English Poetry.* New York: Longman Inc. pages: 31, 57.

Leech, G.N. et al. (1990). *English Grammar for Today.* London: Macmillan. page: 16.

Verdonk, Peter. (2014). *Stylistics.* Oxford: OUP. page:118.

CHAPTER 4

Poet's Profile: Stephen Gill

Stephen Gill is a diasporic, Canadian poet who writes poems in English, Hindi, Urdu and Punjabi languages. His profile that occurs in his poetry book: *Songs Before Shrine, 2007; New Delhi: Authors Press,* is drawn below for reference:

Stephen Gill was born in Sialkot, Pakistan, where he passed his early childhood and grew in India. After teaching in Ethiopia for three years, he migrated to England before settling in Canada.

Poet Laureate of Ansted University, Stephen Gill is an expressive voice of Canada, India and Pakistan. He believes strongly in a democratically elected world government and peace through peaceful means. Global peace and social concerns are the main areas of his interest.

Stephen Gill has authored more than twenty books, including novels, literary criticism, and collections of poems. His poetry and prose have appeared in more than five hundred publications, mostly in Canada, USA and India.

He writes usually in English. Once in a while, he writes poetry in Urdu, Hindi and Punjabi languages. He has also written and published book reviews, research papers on writers and on world peace.

Stephen Gill has received awards and recognitions, including three honorary doctorates; and *Laureate Man of Letters* from United Poets Laureate. Gill has won many literary awards and global recognition for peace, such as:

> *Sahir Award of Honor* from Sahir Cultural Society, Punjab, India; *Plaque* from the World Council of Asian Churches (Canada); Pegasus *International Poetry for Peace Award* (Poetry in the Arts, Inc., Texas); *The Best Poet of Peace Award* for the year 1993 from Roger Cable 11 (Canada); and *The Queen's Golden Jubilee Medal.* At present, he is an Honorary Member of the Ansted University Board of Advisory Council, and a Director of the Children's Aid Society of the United Counties of Stormont, Dundas & Glengarry

> (Canada). He has appeared in several prestigious national and international reference books, including *Who's Who in Canadian Literature, Something About The Author, vol. 63, Gale Research, USA; and Who's Who in Canada...*

On his creative and innovative poetry, more than ninety research papers including critiques by renowned scholars, critics, poets and linguists have been compiled in international anthologies in Canada, India and elsewhere. Gill has been extensively interviewed, and he has expressed his standpoints at great length on the theme of his poems, predilection for symbolic imagery, dislikes for clichés, colloquialism, threadbare metaphors, slangs and abstract, jejune expression.

Gill has described the cruel activities of the fanatic terrorists that goaded him to write his odyssey of agonies and strong protest in his epic The Flame. The poet describes the atrocities inflicted by the fanatic terrorists in these words: "*In the month of February of 2005, I covered a heart rending incident of Honey -a wife from Karachi, Pakistan. Some of her bones had been broken and her nose, breasts and genitals had been bitten* ....

> When the neighbours moved her to a hospital, still bleeding in her unconscious state, her brothers received threats that all the members of the family would be killed and her younger sisters would be abducted and raped if the matter were reported to the police. The news was carried also in Daily Times of February 22, 2005. These and other incidents are the result of the mania of the religious robots.

Eclectic eco-concerns signify poet's strong poetic protests aimed at the inhuman atrocities perpetrated by the fanatic terrorists that he expressed at great length in his epic, The Flame: 2008.

The poignancy of poet's feelings are unfolded in a nutshell in these lines: "*The maniac messiahs open Pandora's Box with the fingers of science and technology, using the muscles of fanaticism to spread the dust of the untold brutalities for the sake of their macabre pleasure. Their path to that domain is paved with the blood of the innocents. The flowers that grow on both sides of the path are fed with the tears of the helpless children and widows.*"

Works cited: Gill's Poetry Books

Gill, Stephen. *Wounds* (1974). Montreal: Vesta Publications.

.... *Moans and Waves* (1989). Montreal: Vesta Publications.

.... *The Flowers of Thirst* (1991). Montreal: Vesta

.... *Shrine* (2008). Allahabad: Cyberwit.

.... *Flashes* (2007, Trilliums in haiku spirit). N.Delhi: Imprint.

.... *Songs Before Shrine* (2008). New Delhi: Authorspress. This collection includes following four collections of poems earlier published:

1. *Reflections* & *Wounds* (1978). Montreal: Vesta
2. *The Dove of Peace* (1989, 1993). New York: MAF Press.
3. *Songs for Harmony* (1993). New Jeresy: Rose Shell Press.
4. *Divergent Shades* (1995). India: Xavier's College.

.... *The Flame* (2008). Montreal: Vesta Publications.

CHAPTER 5

Disgusting Social Ecology

Multilevel ecocide originates from the mischievous human ecology, and malignant human ecology is ingrained in amoral mindset and immoral deeds. *People possessing amoral mindset are not concerned in the least of the norms of right and wrong. They are insulated against the precept of moral values, and they indulge freely in immoral deeds amounting to multifold ecocide. Outrageous human ecology is compounded of disgusting social ecology, depraved political ecology and nasty religious ecology.* Human beings are the products of society. It is the society that makes bad and good persons. The outrageous society of the terrorists disseminates the harmful ideas of hate, violence, trivial fanaticism, enmity and religious animus leading to senseless carnage of innocent people.

In the symbolic poem "The Meechlake Fish" (*Songs Before Shrine*), the poet describes murderous disruption in society caused by terrorists:

With a tail for deliberate ruin
a crocodile of racial disharmony
enters the waters of my land
in the guise of the Meechlake fish.
It plays the waves of life
Fear and ignorance carry now
explosives of confused hatred.

In above poem, the poet has collocated words in violation of the semantic rules of selection restrictions. The collocational rules or the selection restrictions rules require that the lexical items of identical contrastive features should be *"selected in order to form a semantically well-formed combination of two or more syntactically combined lexical elements. (Bierwish, 1980:193)*. Nevertheless, Leech (1978:146) justifies that *"the metaphoric uses of language involve a violation of selection restrictions."*

Every word contains distinctive features, for examples: MAN: GIRL inheres specific features as: MAN: +HUMAN, +ADULT, +MALE GIRL: +HUMAN -ADULT, -MALE

The gleanings of vivid, multilevel foregrounding are elaborated here. The adjectival phrase: *racial disharmony*, having the distinctive features of + abstract, -animate, -count has been pre-modified by a noun phrase a *crocodile* carrying incompatible features as: +animate, +count, +concrete that attracts violation of the semantic rule of selection restrictions, and it amounts to lexical deviation or lexical foregrounding. The lexical deviation is meant for economy of expression and connotative foregrounding of ugliness and fierceness of racial disruption causing a heavy toll of innocent lives.

The peculiar grammatical poetic device of *enallage* is beautifully used by the poet in the newly coined word *muddying*. A.F.Scott (1971:204) defines the poetic device of *enallage* as "the interchange of one part of speech for another, noun for verb, adjective for verb, etc."

The root or base form of adjective *muddy* is suffixed by inflectional suffixing and reconstructed into a contextual verb *muddying* which implies the terrible situation of unremitting defilement of love by hate. The trope of metonymy exercised in the co-ordinate noun phrase *fear and ignorance* presupposes the adverse social situation that timid and illiterate persons have been forced to enter into the evils of murderous hate against mankind in the fiendish role of malignant terrorists. The poem showcases acute situation in social context.

Turner (1977: 236) states that: "The literary writer makes patterns with language but he also fabricates situations and makes pattern of them…The literary situation is not stable but composed of disparate elements or factions producing movement and development."

It is obvious that the poet has violated the rules of traditional grammar to meet the imperative adverse situation. Emotive imagery is apparent in the poem. Abstract nouns (fear / ignorance) are personified, and subtle nuance is embedded in the last two lines of the poem in the sense that innocent persons are coerced to commit the murders of ignorant people.

Explaining the use of stylistics, Turner (1977:239) states that: "Linguist will devise means of describing the subtleties of tone, stress and rhythm in speech, construct ways of revealing ambiguities in syntax and show hidden pattern of association in vocabulary."

Very disgusting social phenomenon is buried in the poem Contemporary Humans culled from *Songs Before Shrine (page-23):*

Desireless of the morn
they are raped
in the desert of solitude
by technology and science.

The word morn is the symbol of peaceful and happy days, while the word raped carrying the multiplicity of meaning suggests that helpless women are molested and their innocent children and relatives are shot dead. *The lexical sets: morn-rape; desert-solitude connote hopelessness and atrocities.*

By means of a rhetorical question, the poet makes a thought provoking inventory of ruins caused by undue, prejudiced war in the poem- A Question culled from the book: Songs Before Shrine (p.49):

If the nuclear bombs drop
will the buds bloom again?
will the birds chirp again?
If the nuclear drops again
will the maidens be wedded again?
will rains kiss the earth again?
If the nuclear bombs drop
will the dawn be born again?
will the players play again?
will the children swim again?

In the above poem, the poetic device of refrain is exercised since the line *if the nuclear bombs drop* appears in each of three stanzas in the beginning, and it demonstrates the suspicious horrors of scientific war. In addition to it, the repetition of modal auxiliary verb *will* foregrounded in the beginning of other questioning lines rivets the attention of the readers to the destructive sequels of nuclear war. Lilting music is composed in the poem by way of the repetitions of the *bilabial plosive* /p/-7times; *alveolar plosive* /d/-3times; *rounded labio-velar semi-vowel* /w/-9times; and *time adverb* again-9times. Assonance appears in the repetition of *vowel letters /a/ in arise again.* Alliteration appears in the repetition of *consonant letters/b/ in buds bloom, be born,* and repetition of */p/ in players play.*

The poem-Humanity, culled from *Songs Before Shrine (p.57),* highlights in symbolic imagery the malignant perspectives of mischievous human ecology. The poem is rich in lexical foregrounding, syntactic foregrounding in that it consists of unusual collocations of incompatible words:

When humanity was crowned
with thorns and hanged

on the cross of dreams
evil birds oozed the blood
from its corpse that rests
now in the grave of aspirations.
Reptiles roam in human form
on the barren mountain of pride
carrying the flag of
their empire of evil.
Traders of dead bodies
are active under its shades.
These dupes need more blood
to extend their borders.
They ooze it now
from blameless citizens
of any colour and creed
by sneaking the freedom of nations
stretching the carpet of their savagery.

The above exemplary poem catalogues the outrageous *lexical sets* of the malignant human ecology of the terrorists. The first two lines: *"when humanity was crowned/ with thorns and hanged"* connote the tragic incidence of the crucifixion of Lord Christ, and these lines reveal the truth that mischievous human ecology has continued since ancient times, and only the tools and techniques of brutalities have changed.

In context of stylistics, *the situation-specific words are called registers. In this poem, varied registers have been used to specify different adverse situations, such as: lexical sets of human evils: pride, dupes, savagery, blood, dead bodies, corpse; lexical sets of politics: empire, freedom, borders, citizens etc.*

Some unusual collocations of words in violation of semantic rules of selection restrictions cause lexical deviations or lexical foregrounding, and such deviations show the figurative use of language.

The poem contains symbolic imagery in abundance. The adjective phrase *evil birds* signifies the sinful activities of the persons of outrageous human ecology who crucified innocent Lord Christ.

The poet advances interconnected situations in that the terrorists of modern times are furthering their evil motives of propagating hate and killing those innocent persons who refuse to embrace their nasty religion rooted in massive hate.

The word reptiles referring to terrorists reflects multiplicity of nuances. Reptiles are cold-blooded animals like snakes, crocodiles, lizards, tortoise that creep or crawl. Terrorists are so timid that like venomous retiles they hide themselves in trenches, and they creep out *works; stylistics is that part of linguistics which concentrates on variation in the use of language, often, but not exclusively, with special attention to the most conscious and complex uses of language in literature.*

Research Design

A descriptive research design is applied to carry out the judicious study of the varied themes prevailing in the eclectic eco-concerning poems.

Sampling

Purposive and judgement samplings serve the purpose of the present descriptive research thesis. Symbolic, metaphoric phrases and the lines rich in eclectic eco-concerns have been earmarked for purposive and judgement samplings selected from different books of the poet.

Data Compilation

The significant poems compiled in and culled from the poetry books of the poet are the genuine sources of the *primary data.* Authoritative reference books on linguistics, stylistics, semantics, aesthetics are *secondary data.*

Data Analysis Techniques and Tools

The technique of stylistics is exercised to explore the primary data relevant to the multilayered perspectives of eclectic eco-concerns concealed in various poems.

The tools of stylistics comprise of *stylostatistics* or linguistic stylistics, *literary stylistics*, and *discourse analysis.*

As a base of primary data compilation, *stylostatistics* enumerates and specifies the lexical sets that showcase various traces of amoral mindset of mischievous people, immoral activities and horrid scenes of ecocide.

Literary stylistics is meant for the evaluation of poet's recurring standpoints, emotive feelings *that relate to eclectic eco-concerns, lexical coherence, emotive cohesion, foregrounding and figurative use of language.*

Discourse analysis is intended to interpret the emotive nuances and multifold issues and poetic protests expressed by the poet in his poems.

Verdonk (2014:4) defines stylistics in these words: "So *stylistics, the study of style, can be defined as the analysis of distinctive expression in language*

in night and entertain the orgy of shooting of innocent, helpless children and peaceful people.

This poem testifies to poet's opinion about terrorists: "*I believe that terrorism, an extreme form of ambition for power to rule others, is the work of organized groups that carry out the bloodshed of innocent citizens to gain political, national or religious power. They disregard human life. (The Flame, 2008).*"

Another significant poem *The Dove of Peace* culled from Songs *Before Shrine (p.8)* is drawn for interpretation. *It treasures various poetic devices, such as: juxtaposition, parallelism, symbolic imagery and refrain.* In the device of refrain, a line is repeated either in the beginning or in the end of each stanza in a poem that hammers the dominant fact in the mind. A few stanzas of the poem are drawn as under:

For a long time
I have been hearing
the dove of peace will be freed shortly
and for that dove's noble flight
a number of carnage waged
numerous men lost their sight
and many more maimed
For a long time
I have been hearing
the dove of peace will be freed shortly
to awaken that dove
today's comfort more sacrificed
our homes now better adorned
with the thorns of hatred...

The three lines that begin each stanza as signature tunes: *'For a long time/ I have been hearing/ the dove of peace will be freed shortly"* forward a promise relevant to the maintenance of freedom and peace, but the outrageous happenings that ensue from false promise expose the terrible human ecology which is meant to satisfy the nasty motives of the terrorists.

Sarcasm, irony of situation, refrain, innovative foregrounding of horrible situation and polysemy or the multiplicity of meanings grip the attention of the readers.

Irony of situation lies in it that the promise of peace is materialised by atrocious temperament. Sarcasm is implied in the warlike arrangements for the sake of preserving peace and freedom. The features of lexical foregrounding and polysemy are analysed as under:

homes (noun): i. features of: +concrete, +count, -human, -animate, ii. dwelling places, nations (connotative meaning). iii. reservoirs of affections, humane feelings (thematic, connotative meaning).

adorn (verb): i. features of: +concrete, +count, -human. ii. cultivate (thematic, connotative meaning).

thorns (noun): i. features of: +concrete, +count, -human. ii. annoying attitude (thematic, connotative meaning).

hatred (noun): i. features of: -concrete, +human, +animate, -count

ii. strong dislike (thematic, connotative meaning)

According to the semantic rules of selection restrictions, the verb *adorn* requires a noun having +concrete, +count, -human features like medals, pictures, flowers, statues but not hatred. The lines *"our homes now better adorned / with the thorns of hatred"* attract syntactic deviation and connote that some nations disseminate violence and abhorrence among people instead of peace, love and fraternity.

In the poem: canto43, part seven culled from the poetry book: *The Flame-p.119,* the poet has stated the adverse social conditions and poor mindset of the forced victims of terrorism in symbolic imagery:

I see a deer chased
by a tiger who is fed
on the flaunting fruits of terror
in the bushes of
unparalleled ignorance
where he cannot hear
the birds of freedom.

The above lines are enriched with innovative animal and botanical imagery to unfold the shameful birth of terrorism. Beautiful symbolic referents are employed to demonstrate the malignant human ecology of the terrorists.

Deer signifies an innocent, timid and moneyless youth, while *tiger* typifies a barbaric supreme leader of the terrorists. Alliterative phrase *flaunting fruits* suggests both very tempting prospects and imposed terrorism. In the prepositional phrase: *in the bushes of* postmodified by an adjective phrase: *unparalleled ignorance,* the semantic rule of selection restrictions is violated which is analysed here. Having the features of +concrete, +count, -human, the noun phrase *the bushes* is deviantly collocated with noun *ignorance* having the incompatible features of –count, +human, +animate, -concrete.

In addition to it, the phrase – *the bushes of ignorance* signifies the crass illiteracy of the youths who are tempted and coerced to indulge in murderous activities of terrorists resulting in ecocide.

The lexical set: *deer-tiger* implies the victimisation of a poor person by a rich, strong person. The other neological lexical set: *bushes-ignorance* presupposes extreme illiteracy.

MAK Halliday, the British linguist, is a precursor of stylostatistics which relates to linguistic stylistics. It focuses on statistical analysis of marked poetic text by way of the segmentation of grammatical categories (noun, clauses etc.) and lexical sets of identical objects and semantic features.

Works Cited

Bierwish, Manfred. "Semantics." In John Lyons (ed.). *New Horizons in Linguistics* (1980). Harmondsworth: Penguin Books. p.193.

Gill, Stephen. (2007). *Songs Before Shrine.* New Delhi: Authorspress.

.........(2008). *The Flame.* Montreal: Vesta Publications.

Leech, G. N. (1978). *A Linguistic Guide to English Poetry. rpt.* New York: Longman Inc. page:146.

Scott, A. F. (1971). *Poetry and Appreciation.* London: Macmillan. p.204.

Turner, G. W. (1977). *Stylistics.* Harmondsworth: Penguin Books. p. 239.

CHAPTER 6

Depraved Political Ecology

The entire world is influenced by the selfish politics of different nations. It is discerned from Gill's poetry that terrorists, as the roots of depraved political ecology, propagate the politics of hatred and mass murders of innocent communities that are not Muslims. Gross selfishness fraught with the maelstrom of bloodshed and massive corruption has become the watermark of modern politics.

An exemplary catalogue poem: Canto-20 that occurs in the book: *The Flame, p.72,* projects the cumulative outrage of the ghoulish, ruthless terrorists which culminates in the carnage of innocent children:

> With jackhammers and chainsaws
> they removed obstacles
> to dig out the nursery
> buried under a pile of rubble.

In the above poem, *the noun phrase,* the nursery, symbolises innocent children that were killed by the malignant terrorists who were obsessed with and overpowered by their mischievous human ecology. When the poet operates the amoral mindset of terrorists, he finds them bad conductors of mercy and they are thickly insulated against affections and love. Little children are but trivial objects for them only fit for killing not for love.

In his significant book, Aesthetics (1985:87-88), Yuri Borev points out that: "The ugly is an aesthetic characteristic of the objects whose natural properties have a negative significance for society at the present level of its development….The base is the extreme degree of the ugly and a highly negative quality. It is embodied in the negative forces which are a menace to humanity….If a man does not control his own social relations, this spells disaster… The category of the horrible includes those phenomena with which man does not feel at ease and which bring disaster and death." Personifying the satanic, malignant mindset, the nasty activities of the terrorists are ugly, base and horrible.

In the poem *canto-31* chose from *The Flame, p.102*, the poet reveals how the terrorists used their dreadful tools of tortures and destruction to compel people to embrace their outrageous doctrines of narrow religion and atrocious, spiteful politics:

Car bombs, mobility and night
have become the toys of the robots
who know how and when
to free their unfed tigers
from the cages of depravity….
Their relentless pursuit
to grab the crown of chaos
swim political pendulums
to promote quick deportations
and wiretapping.

The poem is rich in economy of expression and symbolic nuances. The leaders of terrorism are tagged with title of robots, and in a true sense they are shockingly desensitized human robots. Under duress, they make commitments to indulge in cruel activities of killing innocent people.

Such depraved commitments have depleted them of human emotions as they enjoy the cruel game of shooting innocent children and the youths who disobey to further their terrible pursuits of malignant terrorism. *Unfed tigers* connote the hired youths who are given meal only when they perform the task of killing intrepid people. The *noun phrase: the cages of depravity* carries lexical deviation or lexical foregrounding because noun *cages* having +concrete, +count, -human, -animate features is combined with abstract noun *depravity* of incompatible features as –concrete, +abstract, +human, +animate, count, and such incongruous collocation attracts the violation of the semantic rules of selection restrictions. Similarly, the alliterative noun phrase *the crown of chaos* also violates the semantic rules since a noun *crown* with features of –human, -animate, +concrete, +count is collocated against the rules of selection restrictions with other noun *chaos* having the features of +human, +animate, -count, -concrete, +abstract. It is already clarified that the figurative use of language for freshness of expressions results in the violation of semantic rules of selection restrictions. The alliterative phrase *political pendulums* connote uncertain political tenets.

Another remarkable catalogue poem *"A Man of Today"* gleaned from the book *Songs Before Shrine, p.26* showcases double dealing and deceitful practices adopted by shrewd politicians. A few lines are put in diagram:

SYNTACTIC FOREGROUNDING

Contrastive parallelism of prepositional phrases

Constructive perspectives	*Destructive deeds*
On the one hand	**On the other hand**
Songs for peace>	*<.distribution of weapons*
On the one side	**on the other side**
Refuge for the sufferers>	*<.death from starvation*
On the one hand	**on the other hand**
Slogans for freedom>	*<the nights of cruelty*
Appeals for love>	*<.the fire of hatred*
Crises for unity>	*<.thirst for blood*

The poet has made an effective use of subtle stylistic devices, such as: parallelism, foregrounding of hypocrisy and judicious contrast of controversial adverse activities to unravel the unpredictable and mercurial character of modern shrewd politicians. It is noteworthy that the convergence of prepositional phrases at equal places with ellipsis of subject and verb phrases accounts for semi-sentences. Phrases without verbal groups sustain the urgency of telegraphic sensibilities. Without verbal groups, the prepositional phrases expose effectively the despicable breach of promises by manoeuvring the brutalities of double dealings by the base politicians. *Juxtapositions of peace and weapons, refuge and starvation, freedom and cruelty, love and hatred, unity and blood define the perils of the deceitful and depraved political ecology.*

The remarkable poem-*Canto59* rich in irony and pun that occurs in *The Flame, p.142* testifies to poet's predilection for neologism and his mastery of the coinage of innovative imagery. The clusters of perspectives have been illustrated through lexical deviation:

This is the palace of peace
years of brain-rattling forces
high on a cocktail of arrogance
ignorance and an ideology of sickness
have sealed its doors.
In its kitchen
malice is prepared

Remarkable stylistic features of the poem are analysed here. Beautiful pun shines in the juxtaposition of the alliterative phrase *"the palace of peace"* against the participial phrase *"brain rattling forces."*

Linguistic device *anthropomorphism* is apparent in the line *"In its kitchen/ malice is prepared"* in that the abstract noun *malice* is personified. The *nonce* noun phrase *"a cocktail of arrogance"* suggests an egotistic amalgam of malignant politicians.

It is revealed here that Gill introduces varieties of phrases by means of inventing fresh imagery for the sake of startling use of figurative language although it always violates the semantic rules of selection restrictions.

The poet abstains from using the dregs of expression, such as, slang, cliché, archaism, vulgarism. The poet has put his preferences meant for the niceties of his diction in his book *The Flame (p.8-9)* in these words: *"I am a proverbial enemy of clichés though some are animating and some may creep in without my being aware of them. I believe that a poet should use fresh images."* Similarly, a poem-*Canto15* from *The Flame*, p.60 also contains poignant feelings in symbolic imagery:

Televisions shall not catch
the magnitude of the wounds
nor the agitated reporters
the intense sight
of the repulsive rave.
Distressed by the locusts
from the hell…..

The desensitised, outrageous human ecology of terrorists is manifest in the above poem. *As inanimate televisions cannot be expected to feel the pain of festering wounds, so the inhuman terrorists are not least stirred by the horrible scenes of wounded persons groaning with pain although they are animate persons.*

It is shocking that the reporters get flurried to take the shots of the horrible scenes of wounded persons rather than tending the wounded persons with care. After all, the reporters are paid for the news but not for the welfare activities.

The noun phrase *the locusts from the hell* connotes the crowd of fiendish terrorists that ruins the future of innocent people. Alliterative phrases, *the repulsive rave, the fate of future* render music in the poem in the sense of internal rhyme.

An exemplary poem *Mothers* from the book *The Flame-p99* exhibits how the poet marvels in inventing picturesque imagery for the description of the ineffable agonies of mothers who are bereft of everything:

> Mothers do not weep.
> Shed your tears with cries
> from the skies of your fond memories
> to awake their conscience
> slumbering in the shambles of brutality.
> Offer your hymns to a new birth.
> Your children
> baptized with your tears
> sail on the white wings.
> Dear mothers
> do not unfold the bed of the past
> there are cradles in which
> new babies of aspiration
> are to be rocked.

It is evident from the above poem and others that coining of innovative metaphors is poet's forte. Leech (1978:35) defines *neologism* in these words: *"The technique by which new concepts are introduced is lexical innovation, which takes the form of* NEOLOGISM *(the invention of new words, or more precisely lexical items), or* TRANSFER OF MEANING (the *derivation of new senses of established words)".*

A creative poet does not play with innovative words, but he exercises the technique of novelty of expression. Leech (1978:38) defines metaphor and its importance in these words: *"The metaphor which seems to characterise lexical innovation most usefully is that of a capsule or receptacle or a package into which a particular semantic content is placed, so that it can henceforward be manipulated and shunted about as an indivisible unit of meaning."* The language of above poem sustains the beauty of intimate, persuasive undertones. The texture of the poem rings poet's solace to the aggrieved mothers whose children died in the carnage game of the terrorists.

Aggrieved mothers are motivated to wake by their cries the conscience of the cruel terrorists who take immense pleasure in the merciless killings of innocent children. The innovative metaphoric phrase *"conscience slumbering in the shambles of brutality"* implies many facts: (i) brutality is ingrained in the amoral mindset of the terrorists, (ii) conscience of the terrorists is buried in brutality, (iii) the obsession of brutality has put the conscience of the terrorists into shambles.

It is apparent that metaphoric phrase is an emotive package or receptacle of many perspectives. Similarly, the sentence *"your children/ baptized with your tears/ sail on the white wings"* connotes many situations. In baptism, generally a child is given a name in the Church by sprinkling holy water on his or her head, but the situation differs in this sentence. Children are put to brutal death by the terrorists and their mothers see them off with tears, and dead children go to heaven like seraphs.

In the last stanza, mothers brimming over with agony are tutored to shake off their grievous past, and it is expressed in the symbolic sentence: *"do not unfold/ the bed of the past."* The last lines of the poem connote that mothers should take care of their future that breathes in their other live children.

The neological sentence: *"new babies of aspirations/ are to be rocked"* refers to lexical deviation in that the noun phrase *new babies* having +human, +animate, +concrete features is deviantly collocated with abstract noun *aspiration* having –concrete, –human, –animate features for novelty.

Leech (1978:36) explains the significance of *neologism* in these words: "The effect of neologism is merely to condense into a single word the same meaning that could otherwise be expressed by a whole phrase or sentence". The poet has detailed the merciless, massive killings by the politically motivated terrorists in this catalogue poem: *Canto 22* from The Flame, p78:

> Shocked volunteers
> witnessed a pyramid of ashes
> over the cradles
> a bone chilling calculation
> that demeaned the design in living.
> there was no wailing, no screaming
> over the earth shattering slaughter
> that pulverised the leaves
> of the young season
> untouched by the outburst of cyclones
> Through the openings of the burial cabin
> time differently watches
> the ethical poverty of the zealots
> who frenzied on the wildness of malice.

The above poem is termed as *a catalogue* poem. In a catalogue poem, minute details of any event, great loss, human feelings on massive damage etc., are given.

In the above catalogue poem, the poet has delineated the massive killings of innocent children, mountain of ashes, destructive human ecology of the inhuman terrorists.

The lexical words or content words are subtly systematised, according to Leech (1978:201), through the process of *"semantic-syntactic mapping."* The poetic device of *semantic-syntactic mapping* involves *lexicalisation* in the form of unusual collocation of words for the depiction of unprecedented experience; *structural compression* or verbal economy through elliptical syntax, and *thematisation* or the emphatic ordering of thoughts. The metaphoric phrase: *"a pyramid of ashes over the cradles,"* connotes the nuance of massive murder of infants. The horrible scene of carnage left everyone nonplussed. Symbolic imagery makes the poem very effective. The metaphoric phrase *"pulverised leaves of the young season* connotes teenagers who were slaughtered by the cruel terrorists.

Similarly, the adjectival, metaphoric phrase *"untouched by the outburst of cyclones"* suggests that the innocent children did not enjoy the exuberant energy of youth. The terrorists did not maintain even a shred of morality, but they were overwhelmed with the storm of malignity. They were blinded and maddened by their evil aim of subjugating people to their malignant sect.

Words clothe various patterns of human feelings, ideas and experiences. An appealing patterning of thoughts requires subtle collocation of words, and Gill appears to be a decent connoisseur of startling figurative expressions.

The poem-Canto26 culled from the book *The Flame (page-89)* seems to be a very significant composition in connection with appealing symbolic imagery, lexical deviation or astounding foregrounding of the extremity of brutality and strong rhetorical questioning:

I ask blood spillers
from the cabaret of appalling barbarity
if they hear
the silence of infants
in the cradles of terror;
share the woes of mothers
in the winter of their lives;
see the shreds of peace flying
with the winds of daggers
poisoned in their forts of infamy;
perceive
the twigs wounded

with the kisses of storms;
feel the virginity
of spring losing warmth
to the indifference of cold;
meditate over
the depth of obsessive depravity
that spells disaster
for the birds of freedom.

The above poem is a repertory of incredible brutalities, ghoulish activities of the terrorists, unusual neology and innovative combinations of content words.

In respect of the combinations of words, Boulton (1959:121) writes: "*...all words are suitable for use in poetry, however crude and common, rare or technical, provided that, their associations are appropriate to the context.*"

Addressing the perpetrators of brutalities, the protagonist in the poem reproaches them that they lack human traits of love, peace and affections. Their barbarity has gagged the infants with silence, and the agonies of old mothers do not stir sympathy in them.

Certain metaphoric phrases wrapped in nice nuances reflect poet's commendable knack for neology in regard to the figurative use of language, and the remarkable metaphors are interpreted here.

The metaphoric phrase, *"the cabaret of appalling barbarity"* connotes that the terrorists exercised awesome alacrity in inflicting atrocities on innocent people.

The symbolic phrase, *"mothers in the winter of their lives"* corresponds with the irksome old age burdened with added suffering of irreparable loss of their children.

There lies *polysemy* in the word *winter* in that it refers to cold season, and it symbolises old age as well. Nothing grows in the winter as the earth is caked with snow, and in the same way old age is too cold as it lacks the warmth of young energy, verve and stamina.

Pain harrows life and the old person is treated as a burden on the family in most cases. As a matter of fact, children become the props of the old parents, but the life of old persons becomes more disgusting than hell whose children are killed at the critical edge of senility when they utterly need them.

Similarly, these phrases are clustered with metaphors: *"shreds of peace flying/ with the wind of daggers..."* that contain paradoxical truth.

The persons who unfurled the white flag of peaceful truce were stabbed to death and their attempts for peace were ruined. These lines reveal that the words of peace and mercy have lost their genuine meanings for the terrorists.

Works Cited

Borev, Yuri. (1985). *Aesthetics.* trans. Nataria Belskaya and Yevgney Phillippov. Moscow: Progress Publishers. page. 127.

Boulton, Marjorie. (1959). *The Anatomy of Poetry. rpt.* London: Routledge & Kegan Paul. page. 121.

Gill, Stephen. (2008). *The Flame.* Montreal: Vesta Publications.

.........(2007). *Songs Before Shrine.* New Delhi: Authorspress.

Leech, Geoffrey N. (1978). *Semantics.* Harmondsworth: Penguin Books. pages: 35, 38, 201.

CHAPTER 7

Nasty Religious Ecology

Religion has become an integral part of human beings. People have embraced different religions in different countries. Judicious discussion on the different perspectives relevant to religion is essential not only in context of Gill's poetry but for the benefit of humanity.

In the *Dictionary of Philosophy (1984:357),* the panorama of religion is discussed in these words:

> "The appearance of Religion in primitive society was conditioned by man's impotence in face of the forces of nature because of the low level of the productive forces. The existence of religion in antagonistic class societies may be traced to class oppression, unfair social relations, the poverty and rightless status of the masses, which breed despair and a sense of hopelessness thus turning people's hopes to supernatural forces. Marx called religion *opium for the people.*"

A rational definition of religion also appears in the *Dictionary* in these words: "A scientific analysis of Religion rests on the premise that it is a complex social phenomenon, a system of specific ideas, feelings and religious rites, and in a class society also of institutions that bring together professional clergymen."

It is obvious that the specific systems regarding the establishments of the religious heads and religious rites enshrined in the different scriptures disseminate different religious doctrines that are the root causes of religious animus among the peoples of different nations.

Gill's epic titled *The Flame* is based on the malignant human ecology of the terrorists that is rooted in outrageous fanaticism, and the terrorists foster ingrained hatred against the peoples of different nations that follow ardently non-Islamic religions.

The terrorists are propelled like inhuman robots by their borrowed irrational fanaticism. Poet's eclectic eco-concerns inventoried in his various poems unleash the inhuman bestiality of the fanatic terrorists in very strong language.

Malicious word fanaticism is defined in the Concise Psychological Dictionary (1987:98) in these words:

> "Fanaticism, extreme loyalty to any idea or cause based on blind faith in the truth of one's own judgements and actions. It is accompanied by intolerance of other beliefs and views, and by inability to critically view oneself and one's own actions (like in religious fanaticism)."

In his epic *The Flame,* the poet has expressed the atrocities inflicted on the innocent people by the terrorists who are obsessed by the destructive perspectives of fanaticism. Ideological perspectives refer to a set of social, cultural and political beliefs and values.

Great Indian philosopher late Dr. S. Radhakrishnan (1978:54-55) points out the necessity of religion in these words: "The purpose of religion is to help us grow from this world of intellect, this world of divided consciousness, with its discords, dualities, to a life of harmony, of freedom, of love."

It is apparent that true religion ennobles people to live with love, peace and harmonious relations with others. On the contrary, the outrageous fanaticism of the terrorists is deeply rooted in hatred, spiritual prejudices and merciless carnage of innocent children and peace-loving people.

In the poem *Canto-59* from *The Flame (p.143),* the poet has displayed the deceitful religious practices of the terrorists, and the destructive religious ecology wrought by them:

> Here the litany of the rituals
> unveils the hidden ugliness
> of the inglorious advocates
> of wicked design.

In the metaphoric phrase *the litany of the rituals,* the horrible mindset of the terrorists is presupposed inasmuch as the massive killings of innocent people is regarded by them as their holy prayer. The register (situation specific word) litany refers to the form of prayer for use in church services. *Inglorious advocates phrase* refers to the fanatic terrorists and *wicked design* implies the frenzied carnage by the ugly terrorists.

Lexical deviations as poet's deliberate attempt at neologism are very intricate to be understood by ordinary readers who are unaware of the mechanism of linguistic foregrounding. Hence the poems are interpreted and analysed with the tools of stylistics.

Abrams (2008:72) elaborates some standpoints in that context:

> "It is claimed that the reigning religions and philosophies of Western Civilisation are deeply *anthropocentric*: that is, they are oriented to the interests of human beings, who are viewed opposed to and superior to nature, and free to exploit natural resources and animal species for their own purposes. This viewpoint is grounded in the biblical account of the creation, in God gave man dominion over the fish of the sea, and over the birds of the air and over the cattle, and over all the earth (Genesis:1.26)."

The fanatic terrorists have misconstrued and misinterpreted the Islamic sect by manoeuvring their most nasty activities of willful carnage of innocent children and peace-loving people in the contemptible garb of Jehadis.

Some remarkable poems relating to the nasty religious ecology are discussed here. It is noteworthy that all the poems titled CANTO occur in poet's epic *The Flame*.

The distribution of cantos, specific parts and themes relevant to *The Flame* are discussed in a separate chapter.

All the poems titled CANTO are compiled in poet's epic *The Flame*. In *Canto-28* (page:95), the poet has described the cruel orgies of fanatic mindset of the terrorists:

Here stood
the sanctuary of the lofty art
of tender awareness where
life veiled in ineffable sanctity flourished.
The adherents of a wicked belief
left a dent with the claws
textured in the laboratory of
their conceit
The streets
wandered forlorn for days
while the rubble ached
to shoot forth greenery for new ways.
Indignant waves
of sadness and fury
of every group and race
the patrons of carnage.

It is apparent that the above poem is rich in *neology*, that is, lexical inventiveness, innovative metaphors, metonymy and symbolic imagery that are interpreted here. The poem begins with the decent, peaceful living of common people.

The metaphoric phrase *life veiled in ineffable sanctity* connotes the sinless living, decent affectionate togetherness of ordinary people. Other inventive metaphoric phrases: *adherents of a wicked belief/ textured in the laboratory of conceit* expose the mischievous mindset of the terrorists.

The adjective phrase *wicked belief* signifies coercive measures of outrageous fanaticism that goaded the terrorists to cause carnage of innocent people.

In the clinical metaphoric phrase *the laboratory of conceit* multiple meanings are condensed. Scientific experiments are carried out in a laboratory with glass apparatuses and chemical salts that lack human emotions, and the evil element of mind, that is, *conceit* empties out the mind from humane deeds.

Conceit as a self-centric inclination insulates a person against the spirit of doing good for others. The repetition of initial vowels – *ashes ask* creates assonance, while the repetition of initial consonants – *blind brutes* causes alliteration and music in poems.

Anthropomorphism or personification shines in attributing human qualities to +abstract, -animate, -human nouns *ashes* and *streets.*

The inventive metaphoric phrase *greenery of new ways* implies the view of young generation luxuriant with love, peace, fraternity. The last stanza paints the dull, ugly scene of desolation caused by the carnage of decent people of different nations.

In the poem *Canto-29* (page: 97), the poet has catalogued the disgusting scene of the mangled limbs as a sequel to carnage perpetrated by fanatic terrorists. It is unbelievable, but possible in case of the inhuman ecology of the terrorists, that innocent, amiable people are slaughtered by the terrorists flowing in the cyclone of fanaticism:

Dear children
do not suffer from the painful longing
for the domestic bliss of your early days.
The place
where the dismembered limbs lie
mocks the blindness of the brutes
who had tried to frame a coffin of liberty.
under the shades of
their vilest impulses.
The morning
that buried your elders
in a massive grave of frozen mind

has become a ground of hope.
Locked in obsessions
they briefly stenched the air with
their uncontrolled spiral of hate.

In the above poem, the poet addresses those orphan children whose parents have been killed by the fanatic terrorists. The poet paints a bright future of hope for them. Children are advised not to intensify the agony of their present by recalling the decent days of their bygone childhood. Satiric tone is buried in the sentence embedded with defining relative clauses: *"the place where the dismembered…..vilest impulses,"* because the mangled limbs perform the human task of mocking, but the terrorists are filled with the vacuum of human feelings.

The metaphoric phrase *vilest impulses* connotes the devilish frenzy of fanaticism that drives terrorists to murder those people who fight for liberty and peace.

The last stanza carrying the words *"the morning…..in a massive grave of frozen mind…"* illustrates the beauty of the art of *neologism. Morning* is personified in a dismal sense in that the morning brings death instead of happy message.

There lies multiplicity of nuances in the last two lines:

the metaphoric phrase *massive grave of frozen mind* suggests, on the one hand, that many graves were dug to bury many dead bodies;

on the other hand, it shows that terrorists were completely hollowed of emotions inasmuch as vile fanaticism had sponged out their feelings.

Murderous faith of the terrorists triggers serious concerns in the mind of the poet, and he satirizes the outrageous religion through symbolic imagery in the poem *Canto-59,* p.144:

It is the ruin where
the swords of its pilgrims twinkle
in the wrinkles of the religion
of self-glory.

The above poem is rich in pun and satire. The phrase *the swords of its pilgrims twinkle* implies the malignant, killing kink of the terrorists. In addition to it, the deviant metaphoric phrase *the wrinkles of religion* connotes the extremities of their atrocious religion.

Satire crops up in the combination of the words of counter features: inasmuch as *swords* are kept by the warriors or the soldiers who fight on the front; pilgrims keep scriptures in their hands. *The alliterative metaphoric phrase wrinkles of the religion refers to the misconstrued tenets of religion that equips the sham devotees with an immoral sanction of committing slaughter of innocent children.*

The nuance concealed in the verb *twinkle* implies the import of a twitch of guilt jolting the terrorists for a moment. It is emphasized here that the neological chiseling of words is a studious and judicious attempt, and the interpretation of lexical inventiveness demands expertise wisdom in stylistics which is the part of applied linguistics.

Employing the artistic beauty of neologism in *Canto-27, p.93,* the poet has questioned the incremental hatred of the terrorists widespread in fanaticism:

> Who can tell how they felt
> tormenting the bird of peace
> with the cigarette lighter of their lust
> or the butt of the rifle of their bigotry.

By means of neologism, multiple sentence message is encapsulated in an innovative metaphoric phrase; and it is evident that a large extent of intensive experience can be condensed in a phrase by the process of neologism.

The last two lines are beautified by way of neologism. Very lengthy matter is condensed in the innovative metaphoric phrase *"the cigarette lighter of their lust."*

It is presupposed in this alliterative phrase that first the terrorists raped innocent girls then burnt their thighs to satisfy the irrepressible tormenting urge of their sadistic mindset.

Terrorists culminated in their tortures by pounding through the butts of rifles the heads of people who combated their forced conversion into Islam religion.

The *Canto-27,* p.91-92 is replete with pathos in an interrogative tone. The poet is in keen search of any intrepid person who can wake the cruel terrorists to their savagery of killing innocent children:

> Who can tell
> if the tender hands of the toddlers
> tried to strangle
> the throat of their conscience
> and if they heard the psalms
> of the stars presenting a symphony
> of dignified calm.
>
> Who can tell if the night before
> they tied and untied the knots of reason

before plunging the bayonets
into the raw flesh to appease Beelzebub
with their offerings at the altar
of their seething cauldron of wrath.

Who can tell how
they felt when they concealed
the carcass of their rusted notions
under the rock of the blinding lustres
of the gold of their creed.

Emotive lines of above poem *"the tender hands.....their conscience"* underlie pathos in that the contemptible activities of slaughtering little children did not prick the conscience of the terrorists. These lines also connote that complete indulgence in the evils of fanaticism had eaten up the conscience of the terrorists.

The *nuance* in the wrapping of the metaphoric phrase *"the psalm of the stars"* connotes that the terrorists never got proper education except schooling in terrorism, and they never heard or recited the mellifluous lines " *twinkle twinkle little star...*"

A terrible situation is presupposed in the sentence *"they tied or untied the knots of reason"* that the supreme boss had washed out the reasoning faculty of the terrorists and tamped down terrible ideas of fanaticism in their mind.

The chief of the terrorists on this earth is appropriately hung on the Biblical allusion: Beelzebub. In the *Holy Bible,* Beelzebub is the Chief Lieutenant of the Satan. In Milton's *Paradise Lost,* Beelzebub is the Chief Lieutenant of the Satan among fallen angels who eats little children roasted in the huge cauldron.

The terrorists slaughter little children mercilessly in obeisance to *modern Beelzebub of Islamic States.*

The significant lines *"who can tell......the gold of their creed"* reveal the truth that the young Muslims who were very poor, illiterate and unemployed were allured by the agents of the Modern Muslim Beelzebub.

The Muslim teenagers were assured of immense wealth and other facilities if they joined the training schedules of terrorism programme to advance the cause of fanatic killings of little children and innocent people who refused to embrace the malignant Islamic religion.

A good deal of standpoints are foregrounded in the innovative metaphoric phrase *"the carcass of rusted notions"* inasmuch as the young agents of terrorism cart away their dead soul on the hearse of fanaticism.

Other metaphoric phrase *"rock of the blinding luster"* connotes that the temptations offered to the teenagers were too attractive to be forsaken by them for the cause of the welfare of others.

It is apparent that the destructive creed propagated by the modern Islamic Beelzebub is founded on the plinth of deceitful allurement, coercion, ingrained hatred, irrational massacre and antagonism to other humane religions.

In *Canto-33,* p.107, the poet estranges himself from orthodox rituals of religion, and he reasons the relevance of the formality of devotion:

> I stop counting the beads
> in the cycle of monotony
> for it drops the seeker in me
> Into the well of emptiness.
> I find the artifacts
> of stones and clay
> within the cloistered walls
> of sky-touching domes
> where the waves of human life
> flow once a week
> to bow in silence.

The poet feels that there is no rationality in maintaining the ritual of counting the beads as a part of devotion since he feels hollowness rather than realisation of God in doing so. He does not find the imposing building of the Church as a significant contribution to the enhancement of piety in people inasmuch as they visit Church once in a week, and bow their heads to the Lord silently not in devotion but as a part of devotional formality.

The poem *Canto-34,* p.108-109, reminds the readers the ageless charm of Gray's unprecedented poem: *An Elegy Written in a Country Churchyard.*

Stephen Gill bewails in poignant and symbolic tone over the unpredictable absence of those loving persons that were killed by the terrorists:

> Who shall rise
> to bless the blotless blossoms
> who have lost fathers
> to vultures of the bloodshed

and freshen their withering faces
while swallowing
the crumbs of your absence.
Who shall water
the dreary field of freedoms
turn pages of hope
for battered handicaps
and prepare something
daily for them
on the fire glowing
in the hearth of emptiness.

Gill enriches his poems with neological phrases, innovative metaphors, symbolic imagery and startling nuances. *Nuance refers to a very delicate difference in meaning, sound, colour, feelings that are not usually obvious.* Alliterative metaphoric phrase *"blotless blossoms"* signifies innocent, sinless children; similarly, another metaphoric phrase *"vultures of the bloodshed"* connotes the murderous extremities of the terrorists.

Amazing *neology* is apparent in the coining of an innovative metaphoric phrase: *"the crumbs of your absence,"* in that it is flavoured with a very *subtle nuance.*

Different shades of meanings can be elicited from this phrase:

(i) Noun *crumbs* denotes very small pieces of dry food, especially, a bit of bread or cake rubbed off or dropped from a large piece;

(ii) In figurative sense, it connotes small amount, such as, *a few crumbs of happiness;*

(iii) The noun phrase, *the crumbs,* collocated with the adjective phrase, *your absence,* implies as a *subtle nuance* that only the crumbs of food served by father affectionately whetted the appetite of children, and now they find the food insipid in absence of their father.

A catalogue poem, *Canto-13,* p.53-54 showcases the horrible scenes of mutilated parts of adults and children caused by the maniac terrorists:

The waves of supreme disaster
carried bodies dismembered
with skin sandblasted off.
a man hung out of a window
blood from his head dripping.
A woman moaned on the ground

another writhed in pain with a broken leg.
A short man with one leg blown off
sat looking out of the window
he died soon.
Injured, bloody and burnt
walked panicked and confused.
Wounded kids
were crying on the grass
and broken bodies
discarded like hot dog wrappers.

The horrible and disgusting scenes in the above poem paint the montage of the extremities of savagery, amoral and dehumanised mindset of the terrorists. *The collage of the macabre imagery is analysed here:*

AUDITORY	Certain phrases: a woman moaned; wounded kids crying on the grass etc.
VISUAL	Certain phrases: bodies dismembered; blood dripping head; leg blown off; wounded kids; hot dog wrappers etc.
KINESTHETIC	Certain phrases: a man hung out of a window; woman writhed in pain; injured, bloody walked panicked etc.
OLFACTORY	putrid stench from the dead bodies.
TACTILE	broken leg; dismembered bodies etc.
GUSTATORY	horrible, ugly scenes cause utter disgust.

Analysis of images illustrates poet's linguistic artistry in the sensuous delineation of the aftermath of detestable atrocities of the terrorists.

The poem-*Canto 14,* p.56-58 amalgamates the human rubble as well as debris committed by the cruel and disastrous activities of the terrorists:

A gush of potted plants
steel and concrete
poured down the streets
toys and strollers lay broken
someone found a child's finger.
Angry coal-coloured smoke
shot upward from the place
that bustled with people.
The remnants of wrecked corners
looked grim, the sky wondered sadly
at the mutilated temple pushed
into a grave of unfathomable horror
by the avalanche of hate.

A picturesque description of massive destruction of things and human beings is reported in the poem. Demolition of temples highlights ingrained animus of the terrorists against the non-Islamic religions in addition to their calculated atrocities to disseminate the outrageous Islamic religion.

The first poem – To Mother in the poetry book *Songs Before Shrine, p.1* carries the foregrounding of affectionate pathos manifest in these lines:

Years have gone by still
I see your tearful eyes
and catch the chocking moans
coming from
the crumbling pyramid of pains…
and shroud is spread
on my despair.

Each word is a construct of distinctive semantic features that are contrasted and analysed as under:

Pyramid (features)	**Pain** (features)
+concrete, -abstract	-concrete, +abstract
+countable	-countable
-human	+human
-animate	+animate
-emotive	+emotive
Shroud (features)	**Despair** (features)
+concrete, -abstract	-concrete, +abstract
+countable	-countable
-human	+human
-animate	+animate
-emotive	+emotive

It is obvious that intangible feelings are concretised by collocating the words of clashing semantic features as illustrated above, and abnormal collocations of words account for semantic foregrounding.

Thus linguistic deviations amounting to the figurative use of language serve brevity and novelty of expression.

Lexical inventiveness in the form of semantic deviation connotes that death wrings the soul out of body with ineffable pain; similarly, the vast structures of pyramids are razed to dust with harsh, grating noise.

Shroud typifies the pall of death over despair, and it suggests that the poet presumes himself to be a breathing corpse bereft of mother's affectionate prop.

The poet does not soak himself in exploring the disgusting atrocities of fanatic terrorists only, but he describes the rescue operations in his catalogue poem *Canto-16,* p.62-63 as well:

> Cops on duty leapt from their cars
> doctors and fire fighters dashed
> to set up a makeshift morgue
> where a truck
> refrigerated the slaughtered.
> There were ponchos
> wet weather gear, batteries
> steel-toed boots, hard hats
> hard hats, toilet supplies
> knee pads, dust masks
> tons of snacks as well
> overflow of faith in goodness.

Essential things for rescue operations are catalogued in the poem. A remarkable *nuance* is manifest in the line *"overflow of faith in goodness,"* which connotes that people's faith overflows in the religion of goodness, but never in the outrageous religion of Islamic States.

Works Cited

Abrams, M. H. (2008). *A Glossary of Literary Terms.* New Delhi: Wadsworth Cengage Learning India. page:72.

Frolov. I. (ed.). (1984). *Dictionary of Philosophy.* (trns. Murad Saifulin and Richard R. Dixon). Moscow: Progressive Publishers. page:357.

Gill, Stephen. (2008). *The Flame.* Montreal: Vesta Publications.

Petrovsky, A. V. and M. G. Yaroshevsky (edts.). (1987). A Concise *Psychological Dictionary.* Moscow: Progress Publishers. page:98.

Radhakrishnan, S. (1978). *Religion and Culture.* Delhi: Orient

CHAPTER 8

Decent Nature Ecology

In his odyssey of eco-concerns: *The Flame*, the poet has praised the beauty and significance of nature ecology in the beginning. Thematic categorisations of *The Flame* are specified as under:

Part *One*…*Cantos*: 1-9. pages:32-46. Deification of Nature ecology

Part *Two*…*Cantos*: 10-15. pages:48-60. Destructive activities by terrorists.

Part *Three...Cantos:* 16-18. pages:62-68. > as above <

Part *Four...Cantos*: 19-22. pages:70-79. > as above <

Part *Five*…*Cantos:* 23-25. pages:81-87. > as above <

Part *Six*.…*Cantos:* 26-31. pages:89-104. Accountability of atrocities.

Part *Seven*…*Cantos:* 32-52. pages:106-129. Optimistic perspectives.

Part *Eight*…*Cantos:* 53-62. pages:131-152. > as above <

In his Preface to *The Flame,* the poet has retailed the anecdotes of his ordeals of woes that cropped up from Hindu-Muslim riots.

The poet has unfolded the outrageous mindset of the fanatic terrorists who invent terrible tools of atrocities and derive immense delight from the orgies of slaughter of children and innocent people.

Regarding amoral mindset and immoral deeds of the fanatic terrorists, the poet pours his metaphoric feelings in these words*: "Their path to that domain is paved with the bones of the children and painted with the blood of the innocents. The flowers that grow on both sides of that path are fed with the tears of the helpless children and widows."*

In respect of flame, the poet holds:

> "Flame has been and it still is the main symbol in the Vedic scriptures. In the Hindu religion, the Almighty symbolises five elements. One of those elements is fire. Flame also symbolises sharing, compassion, sacrifice, courage and witness. In Greek mythology, flame refers to the Olympic Flame that commemorates the theft of fire from Zeus, a Greek god, by Prometheus."

Stephen Gill deifies nature in Canto-1 of *The Flame, p.32-33* in exclusive, fine Nature imagery and symbolic metaphors:

You are the imperishable harmony
that reaps unparalleled prosperity
from the chalice of your peace
I long peacefully to sip
the invigorating wine of fruitful returns.
You flower a fragrant feast, caress
the flushed cheeks of the horizon.
You are the distinctive fount
that feeds the ever-growing pangs
of the sages in every age.
You bind the earth and the sky.

Alike renowned transcendental American poet-Ralf Waldo Emerson, Gill too perceives Nature as the manifestation of God. *The fruitful returns of Nature are water, fragrant flowers, life-invigorating fruits, trees, grain-fields and peaceful prosperity.*

Aesthetic beauty shines in the alliterative sentence *"flower a fragrant feast"*, and it implies the luxuriance of varied fragrances of flowers. Inimitable austerities of ascetics meant for realisation of God are presupposed in the metaphoric phrase: *"ever-growing pangs of the sages."*

The poet weighs Nature from various angles of emotions: love, peace, fraternity, morality, graceful attributes like mercy, compassion, sympathy, affections and charity as described in *Canto-2,* p.34:

You are the mother
of the strings of that touch
that cuddles infants
to be carried with cares
to the valley of repose
Your are sickle
that uproots bushes
from the land of ravens.

You are the sincerity of the conviction
that fashions
the necklace of the serene mosaic.

You are the monarch of the ray
that vibrates the carol
of the skylark in flight
and the raptures of
the brilliantly illumined waves
which frolic with banks while sunning.

In the above poem, the poet has perceived the selfless attributes of a caring mother in Nature. As little children take a bath in the sunny affections of a mother, people in the same way lie on the green carpet of Nature to ease out their fatigue and get relief from worries.

A beautiful *nuance* is inlaid in the symbolic, metaphoric sentence: *"You are the sickle / that uproots bushes / from the land of the ravens."* Lexical sets: sickle, bushes and ravens are framed symbolically. *Sickle* signifies a reaper;

> *bush* typifies evil conspiracy, and *raven* (a large black bird like a big crow popularly regarded as a bird of ill omen) symbolises murderous, fanatic terrorists.

This *neological* sentence connotes that Nature's wrath transformed in massive earthquake, severe cyclones, violent flood, drought destroys the evils of people.

Poetic device of circumlocution or periphrasis glimmers in an innovative metaphoric phrase: *"the necklace of the serene mosaic"* that implies the beauty of a rainbow; similarly, the sun is called as *the monarch of the ray.* Periphrasis is a roundabout, intricate way of expression.

It is apparent that the poems as reservoirs of Nature's marvelous grace, afford great delight to all the sense organs of human beings who are endowed with the sagacious faculty of appreciating literature. The poet defines the religion of Nature in *Canto-6,* p.41:

> You are the undying glory
> of the prismatic creed
> that blossoms peace
> on the Maple of compassion
> and the colourful sunrise
> that applauds the dance of the day
> with early glimmerings
> in the valley of plenty
> where diverse streams flow.

The poet in above poem defines the religion of Nature in terms of peace, compassion. The metaphoric phrase *"the prismatic creed"* connotes the impact of essential qualities of a good religion on people which assimilates, like the many facets of a prism, love, sympathy, affection, charity, austerity, morality, selfless service, peace, egoless mindset.

The poet seeks the God's grace for his redemption from the trials and tribulations of earthly life in *Canto-5,* p.39:

> Tell me how to feel
> light fatherly fingers

that shall lift me as a leaf
out of myself to free
my freedoms from
tribes of chaos
and discern the field
that is beyond
common human confines
from where
the vibrating potency
of your sovereign art
heals the corroded minds
who see their god
in the monster of perversities.

The last stanza of the above poem contains one complex sentence embedded with one compound sentence stretched by means of multiple relative clauses.

The poet yearns for a religion that radiates the warmth of fatherly affections, peace and true love. He has entangled himself in the chaotic tenets of differing creeds, and he flounders for redemption.

The spiritual perspectives of differing creeds are not comprehensible to ordinary human beings and they delude people to make life vibrant with peace, love and morality.

The relative clause, *"that shall lift me as a leaf out of myself,"* connotes poet's too much attachments with relatives and endless desires that fail him to realise God. Very difficult it is to pull out the egotistic roots.

Last three lines imply the perverted minds of the fanatic terrorists who perceive God's blessings in slaughtering the innocent children in obeisance to the Beelzebub of outrageous Talibani religion.

December 16, 2014 will be the unprecedented Black Tuesday in the history of inhumanity as Talibani terrorists shot 132 school children in the Army Public School of Pakistan.

Works Cited

Gill, Stephen. (2008). *The Flame.* Montreal: Vesta Publications.

All the poems replete with the detestable atrocities inflicted by the satanic terrorists on innocent children and peace-loving people have been culled from poet's epic *The Flame.* The poems compiled in the epic are not capped with specific titles, but they are crowned with numerical CANTOS: 62 Cantos as stated by the poet in Preface.

CHAPTER 9

Flashes: Haiku Poems

Stephen Gill has composed haiku poems or trilliums also, and he has compiled 252 haiku poems in his book titled: Flashes (2007). Haiku poems are branched out into four sections: *Love, Peace and War, Social Concerns, and Miscellaneous.* The haiku poetic form has originated from Japan, and *Matsuo Munefusa,* 1644-94 well-known by his pseudonym: Basho and *Kobayashi Nobuyuki,* 1763-1828 well-known by his pseudonym: *Issa* were the gifted masters of this form.

Traditional Japanese haikus consist of three lines carrying the specific pattern of 5-7-5 syllables (onji). Japanese haikus are considered to be an offshoot of Tanka, (also known as Waka or Uta consisting of five lines with 31 syllables: 5-7-5-7-7.

Analyzing the subtle style of a haiku, Thomas Sanders (1978: chap.4:55) states:

> "A haiku contains 17 syllables in three lines, each with a set number of syllables: 5-7-5. Other essential elements in each haiku are: a reference to a season of the year, an emotion associated with that season, and an indicated spiritual insight. Brevity demands conciseness, but conciseness is not necessarily syntactical; a haiku need not contain a clause; it may be composed entirely of related phrases or interrelated words creating images."

In essence, haikus appear to be phrasal poems of multifeel, telegraphic sensibilities. Gill's haikus or trilliums lack proper syntax, that is, verb phrases are missing as it happens in the case of haikus.

A haiku contains the attributes of a syllogism. In each haiku, three lines serve specific purposes: the first line, as a major premise, introduces *a proposition*; the second line, as a minor premise, accounts for *the exposition* of an argument; the third line brings forth *the evaluation* of facts. The third line reinforces the thoughts contained in the preceding lines, and it advances a critical nuance which is known as the 'samvegha' or *a poetic shock* in haiku.

Love Perspectives

Love is the most dominant and constructive emotion of human ecology. Some haikus of the poet on the theme of love are discussed in connection with connotative message and inventive style:

Blazing sun
perspiring
I think of you (p.13)

Mostly, haikus intertwine nature images. The metaphoric phrase, *blazing sun* connotes the entanglement of the lover in extreme circumstances, and the lover yearns for the soothing company of his beloved which he misses.

Garden of love
grows thorns
and fine flowers (p.15)

Love is compared to garden to suggest that there blooms varied sweet emotions, and *thorns* connote separation while *flowers* stand for union.

Soul without love
white sepulcher
autumn lurks there (p.16)

It is a significant haiku when construed in context of the destructive performance of the terrorists. Coined in pursuit of neologism, the metaphoric phrase *white sepulcher* suggests that the terrorists as bad conductors of love are but the breathing tombs.

As leaves fall in autumn, so everyone befriends a person who is bankrupt of love. Fanatic terrorists are but *stampeding tombs* on account of their gruesome atrocities of shooting innocent children in school and ingrained hatred for the non-Islamic persons.

A haiku may be a verbal landscape of emotive seasons, but Gill's haikus are emotive montage of human sensibilities and sometimes inhuman sensibilities.

War and Peace Perspectives

As a matter of fact, Gill advocates keenly the cause of peace by exploring the horrors of war and the terrible mindset of fanatic terrorists. It is discerned that the poet strives prudently to beautify his poems with fresh and innovative imagery:

War
buys the blossom of a mother
to slaughter the blossom of another (p.30)

The salient stylistic characteristics of above haiku reflect symbolic nature images employed by the poet. Abstract noun *war* is personified to highlight the trading of poor teenagers into war. Concrete noun *blossom* signifies a young child.

Nuance in the haiku implies that horrible war bereaves many mothers of their children. Young children are led astray by the pinch of poverty, temptations and ignorance.

Eyeless volcanoes
cannons cannot count victims
need soul (p.30)

The above exemplary haiku is clustered with nuances and symbolic import. The metaphoric phrase eyeless volcanoes is wrapped in multiple messages:

(i) plural noun *volcanoes* signifies the terrorists indulged in showering bullets and slaughtering innocent children;

(ii) brimming over with fanaticism, the terrorists are blind to their disgusting atrocities;

(iii) the alliterative sentence *"cannons cannot count victims/ need soul,"* connotes that the task of counting of cannons can be performed by living beings only, but terrorists have turned so insensitive monsters that they focus their attention on the target of shooting innocent, helpless children in proportion to having the stock of cannons rather than counting the shot bodies of children (iv) God did not mean soul for the terrorists like cannons.

In pots of patriotism
poisons are often prepared
to kill lily of peace (p.31)

The metaphoric alliterative phrase *pots of patriotism* are collocated in violation of the semantic rules of selection restrictions in that plural noun *pots* having the features of +concrete, +count, -human, -animate is a deviant combination with abstract noun *patriotism* having the features of +abstract, +animate, +human, -count. The poem connotes that evils seethe in the mind of politicians, and they clip the petals of peace.

Evil kisses nuclear lips
eyes closed
volcano erupts (p.31)

The strope of metonymy in *evil* suggests mischievous terrorists who go blind in using nuclear weapons to kill innocent children and peace-loving people inasmuch as the base terrorists are overpowered by fanaticism.

God daily delivers me
garland of beads
from the buds of peace (p.33)

In the above haiku, the poet has emphasized peace. The innovative metaphoric phrase *buds of peace* connotes that peace comes in piecemeal. The spirit of spirituality breathes in peace of mind and goodness.

Nothing now stands
between God and prayers
bombs have toppled temples (p.34)

Very disgusting mischief is concealed in the above haiku. By means of dropping bombs, even temples are ruined by the terrorists without any scruples. The poem showcases the shocking levity imprinted in the outrageous mind of the fanatic terrorists. It is suggested in the poem that the Non-Islamic prayers and God are good – for – nothing to terrorists.

Social Perspectives

Various social perspectives are patterned in some haikus that are quoted and interpreted as under:

Warm winds
for the bride
new breath (p.25)

Various perspectives are buried in haikus and they can be interpreted from different angles. The above haiku is studied from two angles:

(i) the alliterative metaphoric phrase *warm winds* suggests a newly married couple living together. The bride gets uneasy in the strange but affectionate company of her in-laws in the beginning, but she gets comfort (*new breath*) in the keen love from her husband;

(ii) Brimming over with passions (*warm winds*), young husband and wife entertain intercourse and the wife becomes pregnant after sometime. Pregnant wife delivers a child (*new breath*).

Slum beauty sketched in hall

another begging on streets
shivering under roaring skies (p.24)

In the above haiku, the poet has painted the hypocritical living of rich people in beautiful nature images.

Merely to tone up his pretentious sympathy for the poor, a rich person has decorated his luxurious home with a costly painting which bares the miseries of a beautiful poor girl.

On the contrary, the rich person does not help the poor practically who are begging on the streets and shivering in the inclement weather of thundering cold.

The nuance in above haiku exposes the contrastive deceitful conceit of the rich who showcase superficially their false feelings for the shocking miseries of the poor in paintings only, but they shirk helping the poor with money or necessary things.

Penniless youth
struggling buds
in barren fields (p.21)

In the above haiku, three distinctive metaphors: *youth, buds and barren fields* carry specific situations. Youth are combating the dire problem of unemployment; young girls (*buds*) are fighting against the acute problem of their unpredictable molestations. It is very shocking that government has failed (*barren fields*) in safeguarding the rights of the masses.

Youth in the cage of poverty
thinking of sunny fields
crushed bud (p.24)

The above haiku displays the detestable situation of the youth who are seething with the tormenting problem of unemployment which deters them from achieving their goals of prosperous future (*sunny fields*). The dreams of the youth are razed to dust (*crushed buds).*

She enters the kitchen
fireplace sparkling
flurries outside (p.27)

The poet in above haiku depicts a lady performing her social liabilities gracefully without disturbance (*fireplace sparkling*), although there is much hustle and bustle outside (*flurries outside*).

Marriage is a lawn
to raise
fragrant flowers (p.22)

The above haiku illustrates the truth that the poet has clothed the implied sensuality in symbolic language by exercising the euphemistic Nature imagery.

Nuance in the metaphoric sentence *"marriage is a lawn"* connotes decent relations between husband and wife; similarly, the botanical metaphoric phrase *"fragrant flowers"* suggests nice children endowed with the fine attributes of obedience, great intelligence, due respect and love for parents.

Miscellaneous Perspectives

Haikus concerning with miscellaneous perspectives exhibit the themes of old age problems, individual agony and other matters.

> Old age
> occupants of this house
> searcher warmer climes (p.25)

The metaphoric phrase *"occupants of this house"* contains a polysemy, that means a multiple meaning message. On the one hand, this phrase connotes the repercussions of old age itself; on the other hand, it denotes old people's house. Similarly, the adjective phrase in comparative degree *"warmer climes"* suggests the absence of affections and love at both places.

A distinctive message underlies this haiku that old age has become a tough problem in modern times inasmuch as old people are rebuked variously, and they are deprived of love, affections and respect at home and elsewhere.

> The beaks of birds
> carry gently
> hopes of human love (p.26)

The intra-textual features of the above haiku attracts violation of the semantic rules of selection restrictions in that the action verb *carry* requires a concrete noun, like a straw, crumbs of bread, a fish which a bird can carry in its beak, but the verb carry is collocated with the abstract noun *hope* for the sake of *neology or lexical inventiveness.* The collocation of words of incompatible features causes complexity in the message.

The metaphoric noun phrase *"hopes of human love"* is rich in different connotations in context of others lexical items:

(i) A bird carries something in its beak which is offered by a person who loves birds.

(ii) Some things in the beaks of birds presuppose hopes that love will never exhaust in the hearts of human beings.

Aged fingers
sketching a child
moonless night (p.40)

Haikus maintain disrupted syntax, a little cohesion and abrupt coherence for the cause of packing maximum message in minimum words, and the startling last line happens to be incongruous with the preceding two lines.

The poem is rich in connotations that are interpreted here:

(i) In view of the intra-textual features as well as extra-textual features of the poem, the metaphoric phrase *"aged fingers"* refers to old parents who are discarded by their selfish children even in their old age crisis;

(ii) The improbable activities of drawing the sketches of children by old parents presuppose ingrained and invulnerable love of old parents for their children who live apart with their incorrigible ingratitude;

(iii) The terminal phrase *"moonless night"* implies endless helplessness and dark future of the ousted old parents.

Tormented by insomnia
kitchen cluttered with pills
days awaken malaise-monster (p.38)

The above haiku reveals the adverse impact on the mind of a wife due to her overindulgence in various types of tasks. She suffers from sleeplessness for want of proper rest, and she has had to take various kinds of tablets to do her kitchen chores. The alliterative metaphoric compound phrase *"malaise-monster"* connotes that she feels her body wrecked by pain when she gets up in morning.

Women of today
want pets
no babies (p.36)

The poet satirizes the kink of fastidious women who dislike to beget children, but they are fetish of fondling pets. They delude themselves with a misconception that to deliver a child is to disfigure one's body.

Garbage heavy with bottles
and posters of promises
election over (p.38)

The salient features of depraved politics are explored in this haiku. Deceitful conduct of mean politicians is exposed here. Alluring promises are announced in election campaigns, and voters are offered wine and sumptuous meal by the politicians. Promises are never fulfilled.

Autumn asks
who plants hatred
where flowers go? (p.38)

The poet has introduced the poetic device of *anthropomorphism* in above haiku. Nature is personified in the first line having assonance *"autumn asks."*

Plural noun *"flowers"* signifies the youths whom terrorists killed. There lies lexical inventiveness or clashing collocation in the line *"who plants hatred"*. The poem connotes that Nature herself deplores over the inhuman atrocities committed by desensitized terrorists.

Haikus are not capped with particular titles, and they lack coherence of thoughts. Haikus are enriched through symbolic imagery, connotative construct and abrupt moral in the last line. The following haiku is interpreted from the different angles:

Searching
the fragrance of truth
onion layers (p.49)

(i) The truth is concealed in the heap of lies as the kernel of onion is buried in a number of layers. Great patience and diligence are necessary to explore the truth buried under the mound of false propositions;

(ii) Onions reek of pungent smell that draws tears when they are peeled off layer by layer. The intra-textual and extra-textual features presuppose a lot of troubles that the seeker of truth has had to undergo.

(iii) The seekers of truth are mischievous persons like the stinking layers of onions, and the truth when revealed wafts with fragrance in the atmosphere.

A nice nuance of spirituality concealed in this haiku is interpreted here:

Hidden spring
in withered leaves
sages perceive (p.48)

The above haiku is rich in many connotations analysed in different points:

(i) Poet's mastery of neology shines in each poem. The symbolic phrase *"hidden spring"* presupposes realisation of God by the ascetics;

(ii) The metaphoric phrase *"withered leaves"* connotes skinny body of the sages. In order to keep a tight rein over the urges of their sense organs, Indian sages refrain from taking sumptuous diet and live on fruits. They look like the bundles of bones brimming over with spiritual energy;

(iii) Indian sages detach themselves from mundane affairs, plunge their minds into soul and experience transcendental Samadhi *(hidden spring)*.

Autumn cloud thunder
birds fly
branches tremble (p.46)

In its denotation, the haiku appears to be very simple inasmuch as shows the scene of thundering clouds, the flight of birds and waving of branches in strong wind; but it connotes different emotions.

The Nature imagery stirs many sense organs of the readers:

VISION...	sky, clouds, birds, branches
AUDITORY....	thunder, flight of birds, swishing breeze passing through the branches
KINESTHETIC...	birds flying, branches trembling
THERMAL....	strong wind causing cold sensations
	Viewed from connotative angle, the metaphoric phrase *" autumn cloud thunder"* suggests the showering of bullets by the vile terrorists.

Works Cited

Gill, Stephen. (2007). *Flashes*. New Delhi: Imprint.

Sanders, Thomas E. (1978). *The Discovery of Poetry*. Chicago: Scott, Foresman. Chap. 4:55.

CHAPTER 10

Virtuous Human Ecology

The poet emphasizes on possessing the virtuous human ecology which consists of the attributes of genuine humanism or humaneness. In the *Dictionary of Philosophy (1984:178),* humanism is defined as: *"a system of views based on respect for the dignity and right of man, his value as a personality, concern for his welfare, his all round development and the creation of favourable conditions for social life. Humanism is the opposite of fanaticism, rigorism, intolerance, and disrespect for the views and knowledge of others."*

From the above definition of genuine humanism, it is manifest that the terrorist rackets of Islamic States carry out their atrocious activities on the principles of fanaticism which can be categorised as *the worst pattern of vicious human ecology.*

Man or mind is the monarch of all human sense organs. All the evils originate from man or mind. Man (mind) is defined in *The Dictionary of Philosophy (1978:241)* in these words: *'Man is manifested in the universally recognised principles of behaviour, moral standards, in congealed and materialised forms of language, thought, etc."* It is already stated that terrorists are equipped with an amoral mindset, and it propels them to perpetrate extreme immoral deeds without any scruples.

Amoral mindset means a person who is totally unconcerned even with an iota of good or bad norms.

Human beings maintain some traits of *humaneness.* Humaneness is relevant to the positive faculty of mind. In *A Concise Psychological Dictionary (1987:129),* it is defined that:

> "Humaneness is a system of personality's attitudes determined by moral norms and values to social objects (individuals, groups, living beings) which assumes the form of commiseration and sharing joys in consciousness and activity through acts of co-operation, compassion and assistance."

It is an absolute truth that terrorists represent the worst pattern of vicious human ecology which accounts for multilayered ecocide in that they are depleted of the real traits of *humanism or humaneness* that differentiate man from animal. Globally recognised Indian Scripture – Srimad Bhagavadgita has authoritatively differentiated between a person of divine attributes (Divya purusa) and a person of demoniac traits (Asuras).

In the Bhagwadgita (Chapter 16:sloka-3), the Supreme Lord Shri Krishna explains that a Divya Purusa is born with the divine attributes:

> "*tejah ksama dhrtihi sauchmadroho naatimaanita bhavanti sampadam daivimabhijyatasya bharat.* " (Sanskrit text in Roman English). It means: sublimity, forbearance, fortitude, external purity, bearing enmity to none and absence of self-esteem – these are the marks of him, who is born with the divine gifts, Arjuna.

It is apparent that not an iota of a virtuous person lies in the atrocious behaviour of the terrorists, and they are Asuras.

The Supreme Lord Krishna explains in Sloka-4, Chapter 16 of the Bhagwad Gita, the bad qualities of the Asuras in these words:

> "*dambho darpo-abhimanascha krodhah parushyameva cha agyanam chabhijatasha partha sampadamasurim.*" (Sanskrit slokas in Roman English).

It means: Hypocrisy, arrogance, and pride, and anger, sternness and arrogance too--- these are the marks of him who is born with demoniac properties.

Lord Krishna stresses in sloka-7 other bad qualities of Asura in these words:

> "*pravrittim cha nivrittim cha jana na vidurasurah na shaum napi chacharo na satyam tesu vidhyate.*" (Sanskrit slokas in Roman English).

In English version, the sloka means: men possessing a demoniac disposition know not what is right activity and what is right abstinence from wrong activity. Hence they possess neither purity (external or internal) nor good conduct nor even truthfulness.

As a result, the Supreme Lord Krishna points out the destructive role of the *Asuras* not only in society but in the world in Sloka-9 in these words:

> "*etaam dristimavastabhya nastatmanoalpbuddhayah prabhavantyugrakarmanah kshayaaya jagatoahitah.*" (Sanskrit sloka in Roman English).

It means in English: "Clinging to this false view, these low-witted men of a vile disposition and terrible deed are enemies of mankind, and prove equal only to the destruction of the universe."

The above millennium old prediction by the Supreme Lord Krishna stands true in present scenario inasmuch as the vile terrorists killed 132 school children in the Army Public School in Pakistan on the Black Tuesday: 16 December 2014.

The poet yearns for the enlightenment of the mischievous terrorists by cultivating the traits of humanism and humaneness in their conduct for the harmonious life of peace, love and fraternity in the universe.

Works Cited

Srimad Bhagavadagita, (With English Translation and Transliteration). 1411. Gorakhpur: Gita Press. Chapter:16; Slokas – 3, 4, 7, 9.p. 203-205.

Frolov, I. (ed.) (1984). *Dictionary of Philosophy*. Moscow: Progressive Publishers. page: 178.

Petrovsky, A.V. and M.G. Yarosheevsky(edts.) (1987). *A Concise Psychological Dictionary*. Moscow: Progress Publishers. page:129.

CHAPTER 11

Conclusion

In his significant poetry book: *The Flame (2008)*, Stephen Gill has garnered the rich harvest of the odyssey of his agony caused by the extremely atrocious activities of the terrorists.

Peace, the keynote of his poetry, is disrupted by the mercenary, demoniac venders of death – the terrorists. Flame typifies the surge of exuberant energy in life. Flame connotes the warmth of affections, patriotism, fraternity, wisdom, divine faith etc.

On the contrary, flame reflects murderous perversity, insatiable kink of hatred and unquenchable thirst for slaughtering innocent children in context of terrorists. With a good deal of vile lexical sets, the poet has slashed the outrageous activities of the terrorists.

Pore over lexical sets of derogatory metaphors capping their barbarity: "*monsters of perversity*", "*avatars of savagery*", "*fanatic howls*", "*vultures of bloodshed*", "*snakes of personal migraines*", "*poisonous belligerents*", "*inglorious advocates of wicked designs*", "*sullen zealots*", "*trotting arms savagery*".

It is noteworthy that nobody is a terrorist by birth, but the supreme leaders of the notorious rackets of the terrorists – the ISIS tempt the poor, illiterate children with money, and forcibly trade them into ghoulish activities of terrorism.

In the book: The Art of Happiness (1999:42), appears a significant 1986 Seville statement on violence which was drawn up and signed by twenty top scientists from around the world. The scientists categorically stated that "it is scientifically incorrect to say that we have an inherited tendency to make war or act violently. That behaviour is not genetically programmed into human nature" (human beings grow violent through specially programmed mischievous trainings).

In his book: *The Art Of Happiness (1999:39),* peace Nobel Laureate His Holiness the Dalai Lama, the spiritual leader of the

Tibetan people, writes: "It is still my firm conviction that human nature is essentially compassionate, gentle. That is the predominant feature of human nature (virtuous human ecology)."

On the whole, the poet contemplates the dawn of a religion and the true flame in hearts, minds and deeds of vile people that would kindle true love, peace and fraternity, compassion, and he has sprayed his deep optimism in these lines of the *Canto-60*, p.146-47:

> Where creeds are not crushed
> and human gods do not feed
> the vultures of war
> that island of yours
> defends the dignity of freedoms
> that are distinctive and charming.

The poet makes sincere efforts through his strong poetic protests to revive virtuous human ecology to prevent multilayered ecocide. It is noteworthy that the existence of all living beings depends upon the safety, nourishment and preservation of Nature ecology in addition to enlightening the flame of peace, everlasting love and fraternity.

The survival of Nature ecology and the revival of virtuous human ecology require in true spirit the replacement of anthropocentrism by *ecocentrism.* In this connection, Abrams (2008:73) writes: "*A present day counter movement, sometimes named "deep ecology," maintains that all attempts to reform particular instances of the spoliation of the natural world deal with symptoms rather than the root cause, and that the only real hope of is to replace anthropocentrism by ecocentrism: the view that all living things and their earthly environment, no less than human species, possess importance, value, and moral and political rights.*"

The remarkable thoughts of H.H. the Dalai Lama (1999:47) are noteworthy and commendable:

> "The purpose of our life needs to be positive. We weren't born with the purpose of causing trouble, harming others. For our life to be of value, I think we must develop basic human qualities---warmth, kindness, compassion. Then our life becomes meaningful and more peaceful---happier."

The poet articulates his strong poetic protests against the vicious and outrageous human ecology of the fanatic terrorists that is fraught with hatred, disgusting drive for the slaughter of innocent children and violent imposition of their murderous religion of the notorious Islamic States on the rest of the nations in the world.

The poet prays for the virtuous human ecology which is rich in compassion, true love, peace and fraternity without death harvesting in the name of religion. All over the world, human beings must imbibe pragmatically and follow the preaching of the Upnishads in true spirit:

"Asato ma sadagamaya":	O God, take me away from evils to virtues.
"Tamaso ma jyotiragamaya":	O God lead me from the dark path of evil deeds to the bright path of the virtuous deeds.
"Vasudhaiva kutumbkam":	The entire world is my family.

Works Cited

Abrams, M. H. (2008). *A Glossary of Literary Terms.* New Delhi: Wadsworth Cengage Learning. page: 73.

Gill, Stephen (2008). *The Flame.* Montreal: Vesta publications.

Lama, H H Dalai and Howard C. Cutler, MD. (1999). *The Art of Happiness.* London: Hodder and Stoughton. pages: 39,42,47.

Bibliography

Primary Sources

Poetry Books by Stephen Gill

Gill, Stephen. *Wounds.* Montreal: Vesta Publications. 1974.

.........*Moans and Waves.* Montreal: Vesta Publications. 1989.

.........*The Flowers of Thirst.* Montreal: Vesta Publications.1991.

.........*Flashes (trilliums in Haiku spirit).* New Delhi: Imprint.2007.

..........*Shrine.* New Delhi: Authors Press. 2008.

.........*Songs Before Shrine.* New Delhi: Authors Press. 2008.

Songs Before Shrine poetry book includes following four collections published earlier:

1. *Reflections and Wounds.* Montreal: Vesta Publications. 1978.
2. The Dove of Peace. New York: MAF Press. 1989/ 1993.
3. *Songs of Harmony.* New Jeresy: Rose Shell Press. 1993.
4. *Divergent Shades.* India: Xavier's College. 1995.

Gill, Stephen. *The Flame.* Montreal: Vesta Publications. 2008.

Secondary Sources

(*Citations of authors culled from the following Reference Books on Linguistics, Stylistics, Semantics, Literature are introduced among the texts to substantiate the significant standpoints of the researcher*):

Abrams, M. H. *Glossary of Literary Terms.* New Delhi: Wadsworth Cengage Leaning. 8th ed. 2008. Print.

Bierwish, Manfred. "Semantics." In John Lyons (ed.). *New Horizons in Linguistics.* rpt. Harmondsworth: Penguin Books. 1980. Print.

Borev, Yuri. *Aesthetics.* Moscow: Progress Publishers. 1985. Print.

Boulton, Marjorie. *The Anatomy of Poetry.* rpt. London: Routledge & Kegan Paul. 1959. Print.

Chomsky, Noam. *Aspect s of the Theory of Syntax.* Cambridge. Mass: M I T Press. 1965. Print.

Eisenberg, E. *Ecology of Eden.* New York: Alfred Knopf. 1998. Print.

Frolov, I. *Dictionary of Philosophy.* Moscow: Progress Publishers. 1984. Print.

Gleason, H. A. *Linguistics and English Grammar.* New York: Holt, Rinehart & Winston. 1965. Print.

Glotfelty, C. and Harold From (Eds.). *The Ecocriticism Reader: Landmarks in Literary Ecology.* Athens and London: University of Georgia Press.1996. Print.

Haggett, Peter. "Human Ecology." In Bullock, A. Stallybrass, O and Trombley, S. (Eds.). *The Fontana Dictionary of Modern Thought.* 2nd ed. London: Fontana. 1988. Print.

Lama, H H Dalai and Howard C. Cutler MD. *The Art of Happiness.* London: Hodder and Stoughton. 1999. Print.

Leech, G.N. *Semantics.* Harmondsworth: Penguin Books. 1978. Print.

.... et al. *English Grammar for Today.* London: Macmillan. 1990.

.... *A Linguistic Guide to English Poetry.* Twelfth imp. New York: Longman Inc., 1987. Print.

Meeker, J. *The Comedy of Survival: Literary Ecology and the Play Ethic.* 3rd ed. Tuscon: University of Arizona Press. 1997. Print.

Mellanby, Kenneth. "Ecosystem." In Bullock, A et al (Eds). *The Fontana Dictionary of Modern Thought.* 2nd ed. London: Fontana. 1988. Print.

Petrovsky, A.V. and M.G. Yaroshevsky (Eds.). *A Concise Psychological Dictionary.* Moscow: Progress Publishers. 1987. Print.

Preminger, Alex et al (Eds.) *Princeton Encyclopedia of Poetry and Poetics.* 6th rpt. London: Macmillan Press. 1986. Print.

Radhakrishnan, S. *Religion and Culture.* Delhi: Orient Paperbacks. 1978.

Sanders, Thomas E. *The Discovery of Poetry.* Chicago: Scott, Foresman. 1978. Chpt. 4:55. Print.

Scott, A.F. *Poetry and Appreciation.* rpt. London: Macmillan. 1971.

Srimad Bhagavad Gita. (English translation and transliteration) 1411. Gorakhpur: Gita Press. 2010. Print.

Turner, G.W. *Stylistics.* rpt. Harmondsworth: Penguin Books. 1977.

Verdonk, Peter. *Stylistics.* Oxford: OUP. 2014. Print.

Appendix

(A) Papers Published in International Refereed Journals:

1. Title: STYLISTIC DYNAMICS OF KK SRIVASTAVA'S POETRY

   Journal: **Labyrinth:** Vol.4/ No.1.: January 2013. ....109-115.

   I S S N: 0976-0814 (pages: 158-62).

2. Title: APPRAISAL OF ECO-CONCERNS IN STEPHEN GILL'S POETRY.

   Journal: **Glimpses:** Vol. 2. No.2.: June, 2013. ....116-128.

   I S S N: 2250-0561 (pages:01-11).

3. Title: STUDY OF PERVERSE HUMAN ECOLOGY IN STEPHEN GILL'S POETRY.

   Journal: **B i z z B u z z:** Vol.16.: October, 2013. ....129-139.

   I S S N: 2277-8896 (pages: 30-38).

(B) Papers Presented in International Conferences:

1. Paper: LINGUISTIC CREATIVITY IN POETRY............140.

   Conference: *International Conference on Empowering English Language Classroom.*

   Convener: Malviya National Institute of Technology (MNIT).

   Place: Jaipur (Rajasthan).

   Date: 18th -19th J a n u a r y 2013.

2. Paper: TECHNIQUES FOR OPTIMIZATION OF COMMUNICATION

   Conference: *International Conference on Technical Innovations*...141

   Through Modern Engineering Sciences: TIMES-2013.

   Convener: Institute of Engineering & Technology (I E T)

   Place: Alwar (Rajasthan).

   Date: 23-24 February 2013.

(C). Bio-Data of Nar Deo Sharma

Qualifications

(i) M.Phil (Linguistics).

(ii) Post Graduate Diploma in Teaching of English (PGDTE): CIEFL (Hyderabad), Equivalent to M. Phil.

(iii) M. A. (English Literature).

(iv) LL. B.

Publications

(i) *Melody of Wounds* (1984, rpt. 2007): Poetry book.

(ii) *Emotionoceans* (2015): Poetry book.

(iii) *Style in the Manneristic Poetry: Flickers* (1995): Monograph on Literary Stylistics.

Papers Published in International Refereed Journals

1. Indian English Poets: 1980-85. *Language Forum, Delhi.* Vol. 12. No. 14.

   1986 pp. 37-51. ISSN 0253-5071.
2. Study of Image Motifs in Indian English Poetry. *Poetcrit,*

   Maranda(HP): January 2012. Vol. xxv. pp.166-71. ISSN O97O-2830.
3. Appraisal of Eco-concerns in Stephen Gill's Poetry. *Glimpses,*

   Meerut(UP). Vol, 2. June 2013. pp. 1-11. ISSN 2250-0561.
4. Study of Perverse Human Ecology in Stephen Gill's Poetry. *Bizz*

   Buzz. Bangalore. Vol.16. 2013. pp. 38-45. ISSN 2250-0561.

Papers Presented in International Conferences, Seminar

1. Innovative Ways of Strengthening Vocabulary (Paper Title).

   6th International and 42nd ELTAI Conference on Teacher Development (theme)

   Organised by VIT University, Vellore with British Council: 16-18 June 2011.
2. Perspectives of Untranslatable Lexical Items. (Paper Title).

National Seminar on Redefining the Nation Through Translating Bhasha Literatures: Problem and Perspectives.(theme).

Organised by DAV (PG) College, Deharadun (Uttara Khand) under the aegis of UGC, ICSSR.

17-18 January 2012.

3. Linguistic Creativity in Poetry. (Paper Title).

   International Conference on Empowering the English Class Room (theme).

   Organised by Malviya National Institute of Technology (MNIT) Jaipur.

   18-19 January 2013.

4. Techniques for the Optimization of Communication. (Paper Title).

   International Conference on Technical Innovations Through Modern

   Engineering Sciences: T I M E S 2013. (theme).

5. *Organised by I E T College, Alwar under the aegis of Earth Sciences Delhi.*

   23-24 January 2014.

Papers Published in National Anthologies

1. Significance of Foregrounding in Stephen Gill's Poetry. In-*Essays on the Poetry of Stephen Gill.* Edited by Dr. Shaleen Kumar Singh.

   Adhyayan Publishers, New Delhi.2010. pp.1-16.

   ISBN 978-81-8435119-4.

2. Perspectives of Untranslatable Lexical Items. In-*Nation Translation and Bhasha Literatures.* Edited by Dr. Harbir Singh Randhava. Sarup

   Book Publishers, New Delhi. 2013. pp.257-58.

   ISBN 978-81-7625-908-8.

3. Formulaic Styles in Women Writings. In-*The Cocktail Book of English Literature.* Eds. Dr. Satendra Kumar and Dr. Archana Tyagi. Yking

   Books Publishers, Jaipur. 2014. pp.111-18. ISBN 978-93-82532-49-1.

4. Explorations of Swami Nem Pal's Poetry. In-*Critical Ruminations on the Literary Works of Swami Nem Pal.* Edited by Dr. Shaleen Kumar.

   Madhu Publications, Budaun.2012.pp.1-11.ISBN 978-81-907258-9-7.
5. Appraisal of Eco-concerns in Stephen Gill's Poetry. In – *Insight: A Compendium of World Literature.* Eds. Dr. Manoj and Dr. Satendra.

   Ykings Books, Jaipur. 2014. pp.135-48. ISBN 978-93-82532-50-7.

Poetry in Anthologies

1. Voices from Within: Berhampur, Orissa.
2. Dayspring: Ranchi, Bihar.
3. Heaven: Michael Madhusudan Academy, Calcutta.
4. Prevalent Aspect in Indian English Poetry: Khanna, Punjab.
5. Indian English Writing: Bahri Publications, New Delhi.
6. Interviews with Indian English Poets by Dr.Atma Ram, Calcutta.
7. The Silence Within: Published by International Library of Poetry, Owings Mills, USA.
8. Journeys: A World Anthology of Poetry, South Africa, 2009.

Literary Awards

1. *Femina Poetry Contest Commendation Award.*
2. *Skylark International Poetry Runner-up Prize.*
3. *Distinguished Thinker and Poet Award.*

Biodata in International Reference Books

1. *International Who's Who in Poetry, Cambridge (UK).*
2. *Men of Achievements, Cambridge (UK).*
3. *Who's Who in the Commonwealth, Cambridge (UK).*
4. *Dictionary of International Biography, Cambridge (UK).*
5. *International Directory of Distinguished Leadership, USA.*
6. *International Register of Biographies, USA.*
7. *The International Book of Honor, USA.*
8. *A Dictionary of Indian English Litterateurs, India.*

Fellowships/Memberships

1. World Academy of Poets, Cambridge (UK).
2. English Language Teachers Association of India, Chennai.
3. International Association of Teachers of English as a Foreign Language, IATEFL, Kent (England).

Index